Straits Chinese
BEADWORK &
EMBROIDERY
A Collector's Guide

Ho Wing Meng

Times Books International
Singapore ● Kuala Lumpur

Note on Romanization

In this third volume in the series **The Straits Chinese Heritage**, we have switched to the Pinyin system of romanization. Empress Dowager Tzu Hsi is now Empress Dowager Cixi, Chou dynasty is now Zhou dynasty, and Chekiang now appears as Zhejiang. We have however decided to retain the older names of Canton and Amoy for the sake of familiarity to readers.

Photography: Hong Tiong Peng
Design: Jenny Soh

© 1987 TIMES BOOKS INTERNATIONAL
Times Centre
1 New Industrial Road
Singapore 1953

Lot 8238 Jalan 222
46100 Petaling Jaya
Selangor
West Malaysia

Printed by Kyodo-Shing Loong Printing Industries Pte Ltd

ISBN 9971 65 194 7

For
Fui Len

Contents

Preface

I should like to state here that in this work which is purportedly intended to be an appreciative description and evaluation of Straits Chinese beadwork and embroidery of a bygone era, I have not adhered rigidly to the unstated but orthodox principle of scientific writing. According to this tradition of writing – even when applied to humanistic studies – the writer is expected to maintain an unvarying attitude of objective neutrality, by presenting facts and data as they are without allowing irrelevancies and digressions of any sort, such as reports of anecdotal or episodic experiences and expressions of personal opinions to intrude one's narrative. The implicit assumption here is that by strictly observing the principle of scientific reporting, one is able to achieve clarity and precision in the presentation of facts by eliminating the element of personal bias from one's account.

Like most people, I recognize the value of objective description and analysis in all my works. Nevertheless, I have not hesitated to deviate from it whenever I believe a more insightful understanding could be gained by, for example, viewing some cultural and historical artefact evaluatively in terms of the role or roles which it plays in the customs, the tastes and the tradition of the people (in this case, the babas and nonyas of the former Straits Settlements) for whom it was made. This style of narrative in terms of historical, cultural and aesthetic explanations is, perhaps, not scientifically acceptable. For one thing, it makes no pretension at offering explanations which are logically tied to predictions and the testings of hypotheses. Indeed, the alert reader will probably notice that interwoven into certain parts of my narrative are statements of fact, fiction and conjectures. But it is none the worse for that. For the inclusion of fiction and conjectures is not intended to mislead the unwary reader into mistaking them for true propositions, but rather, to arouse his interest and imagination, and where possible, to whet his appetite for making further inquiry of his own.

Acknowledgements

The preparation of this work for publication has taken a long time to bear fruit, with many interruptions along the way. It went back to 1974 when I first formed the idea of writing a book on the beadwork and embroidery of the former generations of Straits nonyas. But for some reason or other, two other companion volumes to this work, namely, *Straits Chinese Silver* (1st and 2nd editions) and *Straits Chinese Porcelain*, as well as a number of articles on philosophical and semi-philosophical topics, were published before I could find time to work on various drafts of this manuscript. For an academic who spends most of his life in teaching, research and administration in the university, finding the time to write about Fine Art could at best be described as an intellectual diversion. Thus the long gestation of this work.

I am indebted to the authorities of the former University of Singapore for granting me a five-month sabbatical during the summer of 1978 to work in the British Library, London. There I was able to divide my time between consulting the literature on beads and embroidery, and reading the writings of Sir Karl Popper and Michael Polanyi. I thank the Trustees of the British Library for permission to consult their enormous collection of rare and important books.

Mrs Grace Saw deserves special thanks for allowing me to study at my leisure her incomparable collection of Straits Chinese beadwork and embroidery, and in granting permission to reproduce some of the choicer pieces in her collection for inclusion in the illustrations of this book.

Mr Peter Wee of Katong Antique House has been unfailingly generous in allowing me free access to his personal collection of beadwork and embroidery. And he was only too willing when I asked for permission to include some of his pieces in the illustrations.

I wish to thank Mr Wee Guan Hong and particularly his wife, Mrs Josephine Wee, for allowing me to include several of Mrs Wee's *kebayas* and *sarungs* in the illustrations.

Mr Donald Harper willingly offered his unique pieces of beadwork and embroidery specially collected from various parts of Indonesia, and which were presumably fabricated by the former generations of Indonesian nonyas, for inclusion in this work. I take this opportunity to express my appreciation to him.

I want to thank Mr Gwee Thian Hock, William and his mother, Mrs Gwee Peng Kwee, for educating me on some of the finer and more recondite aspects of the Straits Chinese culture, and for permission to reproduce the wedding photograph of Mr and Mrs Gwee Peng Kwee.

To Miss Winnie Yap and Mr Willie Yap, old friends of ours, I wish to express my thanks for presenting us with the wedding photograph of their late parents, Mr and Mrs Yap Kim Swee, and for allowing us to reproduce their photograph in the text.

Miss Rosna Buang worked tirelessly to decipher my ugly handwriting by using the word processor to type out the entire manuscript at least twice over. I am naturally very grateful for her efforts.

Mr Albert Teo took copious notes for me on several occasions when I was making detailed observations and commentaries of beadwork and embroidery in various private collections. He deserves a note of thanks.

To my mother who first awakened my appreciation for the beauty and glorious colours of her own embroidered handiwork, I am ever grateful for the memory of those early childhood years.

Finally, my wife, Fui Len, deserves a special note of thanks for all the trouble she went through to help me secure permission from various friends and acquaintances to allow us to view their personal collections. Fui Len was actually among the earliest people I know, who took a real interest in the beadwork and embroidery of the bygone generations of nonyas. This work is written for her as a token of my appreciation.

The credit for this work is largely attributed to the efforts of many people who have helped me in one way or another. The faults and shortcomings are entirely mine.

1
Introduction

A S THE TITLE suggests, this volume is divided into two sections, namely, Straits Chinese beadwork, and Straits Chinese embroidery. It is not normally recognized by most students of Straits Chinese culture, that with the exception of perhaps the distinctive art of nonya cooking, *nonya* beadwork and embroidery (and I use the term *nonya* to qualify beadwork and embroidery advisedly) are the only categories of Straits Chinese decorative arts which may truly be described as indigenous to the culture. Not only were these articles of beadwork and embroidery fabricated in typically Straits Chinese taste (i.e. ornateness of design, brilliant display of colours and finely wrought workmanship), but more importantly, they were the handiwork of the nonyas of nineteenth-century British Straits Settlements.

Whereas their distinctive porcelain wares, gold and silverwork, batik *sarungs* and embroidered *kebayas* (to a lesser extent), and even their eclectic styles of European-Chinese architecture, had been created for them by skilled artisans, potters, weavers, craftsmen, carpenters and building contractors of non-Straits Chinese origin, their beadwork and embroidery were almost exclusively fabricated by the nonyas. In this sense, they may be said to express more authentically the spirit and character of Straits Chinese culture than all the verbal avowals and pronouncements concerning their customs and beliefs.

Some people may baulk at the suggestion implied here, that these humble mementoes of two, or perhaps three, categories of 'minor arts', can possibly provide us with useful and essential insights into the culture. On the face of it, this skepticism is perhaps justified. After all, we generally look to the social, political and economic institutions rather than such petty and inconsequential things such as the arts and crafts of a community, in order to glean important information concerning the characteristic qualities of its people. By and large most people are inclined to think that the characteristic of a nation or community is best read and understood in books describing their history, and social, economic and political institutions.

Kenneth Clark, the distinguished art historian and critic, attributed to John Ruskin who is reputed to have said:

> 'Great nations write their autobiographies in three manuscripts, the book of their deeds, the book of their words and the book of their art. Not one of these books can be understood unless we read the two others, but of the three the only trustworthy one is the last.'

Sir Kenneth goes on to say that when writers, propagandists and politicians come out with all sorts of edifying sentiments and pronouncements in the form of political manifestos of one sort or another, it is normal to regard them as no more than declarations of intent. 'If I had to say which was telling the truth, a speech by the Minister of Housing, or the actual building put-up in his time, I should believe the building.'[1]

And I suppose the same could be said about some of the current efforts given to describing and theorizing about Straits Chinese culture, except that the babas themselves have written practically nothing about the book of their deeds, the book of their words (which may be construed as their historical, literary, poetical works, if any), or even the books of their arts (until the last ten years or so).

After the era of great prosperity from about the middle to the end of the nineteenth century during which the Straits Settlements was under British colonial rule, the decline of the Straits Chinese community really began with the Great Depression of 1930 to 1934. Indeed, many older babas and nonyas whom I had interviewed over the years, traced the rapid decline of their family fortunes to the period of the Great Depression, when their family business enterprises were forced into bankruptcy by banks and other creditors attempting to recall outstanding loans and overdrafts.

The Depression was followed by a brief spell of consolidation and development up to about the end of 1941. Then came the invasion and conquest of Malaya and Singapore by the Japanese in 1942. From then on, until Malaya and Singapore gained political independence in 1957 and 1965 respectively, the decline of the Straits Chinese community and its unique way of life was so far gone, that most baba-nonyas in Singapore, Malacca and Penang abandoned the majority of their cherished customs and traditions. Thus, as a community with a distinctive culture, they were in danger of being totally eclipsed by the tide of nationalism and modernization, until about 1975 or thereabouts, when public interest in Straits Chinese culture was revived by a surge of publicity

in local newspapers concerning nonya cuisine, the peculiarities of their customs, especially the wedding customs and their cultural artefacts. Until then, it was rare indeed to meet with babas who openly identified themselves as babas rather than as 'people of Chinese origin'.[2]

Nevertheless, despite the commendable efforts of babas and nonyas who have come out of long seclusion to become writers, *pantun* singers, nonya cooks, playwrights, actors in modern versions of *bangsawan* operas, or even the revival of the custom of wearing *sarung kebaya* and *baju loksuan* on ceremonial occasions, the days of the Straits Chinese community seem to be numbered. Thus, when the present generation of elderly babas and nonyas passes from the scene, the only tangible things which remain would be these mementoes from the books of their needs – their arts.

Since the Straits Chinese culture is conspicuous for its absence of a body of literary, social, political, historical, poetic and dramatic resources even though it possessed a spoken and written language in Baba Malay, it is to their arts and crafts which we must turn to for a reconstruction and understanding of some essential features. In the two previous volumes of this series on Straits Chinese Heritage, namely, *Straits Chinese Porcelain* and *Straits Chinese Silver*, I described the characteristic features of these artefacts against the background of the various customs and traditions which determine their functions, their forms and the kinds of motifs appropriate to them. This volume is written in the same spirit and with the same assumption.

As one gets to know these surviving pieces of beadwork and embroidery better, one realizes that they exhibit certain features which, in a fundamental sense, define more explicitly Straits Chinese tastes in all their arts and crafts. In particular, there is this fondness for bright and variegated colours, richness of texture, ornateness of decorative designs, refinement of workmanship

Fig. 1 Details of a beaded panel executed entirely by the technique of threading small Rocaille beads. Some of the beads used by former generations of Straits nonyas were as tiny as 0.5 mm. The design here shows a spray of blossoming peonies depicted somewhat like roses – a characteristic of the draughtsmanship of Penang nonyas. The zig-zag turquoise background in two shades of blue-green provides a particularly striking contrast to the red, yellow and green of the floral sprays. This fondness for rich colours and texture was a universal characteristic of the Straits Chinese. From Penang. Collection of Mrs Grace Saw.

Fig. 2 This complex but colourful, silk embroidered-cum-beaded set of panels is another example of the richness and colourful complexity which characterizes the beadwork and embroidery of the Straits Chinese of the last century. The rectangular panel at the top, depicting three peony blossoms and a pair of birds, is fabricated by the seed stitch and gold thread couchings. The second panel, made entirely out of threaded beads, shows a different variation of the design on the upper panel. The bottom of this panel is trailed by long tassels of strung beads. Artefacts of this sort were meant to be used as a decorative cover for the bridal dressing mirror. Probably late nineteenth century. From Penang. Collection of Mrs Grace Saw.

Fig. 3 Objects of virtu fabricated entirely out of stitched Rocaille beads. The three articles shown here are a blue wedding purse with the design of a cock, a powder box (?) with two cylindrical receptacles for hairpins (?), and a spectacle case. Properties of Mr Peter Wee and Mrs Ho Wing Meng.

and objects of virtu, especially in beadwork and embroidery. Some of their finest artefacts have a jewel-like quality about them. And yet, for all the scintillating colours and complex intricacies of design, the general form or structure of any artefact made to Straits Chinese taste, is always simple and free of any grotesque contortions. Thus, a necklace is always recognizable as such, and so are pillow and bolster ends, wedding slippers, head-gear, ceremonial collars, etc. Since beadwork and embroidery were the handiwork of the nonyas themselves, Straits Chinese connoisseurship is probably nowhere better expressed than in some of the artefacts illustrated here (see figs. 1 & 2).

We know that the nonyas will never again create those lovely pieces of beadwork with their subtle and complex designs, nor for that matter, those small but precious-looking pieces of embroidery with their wonderful sense of colour and mastery of fine and ingenious stitches, some of which are shown in this volume (see figs. 3, 4 & 5). This is because the traditional way of life, as manifested in their quaint and colourful wedding customs and which required their womenfolk to work endlessly at stitching, stringing, and threading those objects of virtu that many people have come to prize so highly nowadays, became obsolete at least fifty years ago. The prospect that the younger and more modern nonyas of today would revive these arts without the backing of an authentic cultural milieu, is simply remote.

And mindful of the fact that the hot and humid

Fig. 4 This exceptional piece of circular table-cover, about three feet in diameter, was created with nothing more than a simple iron needle, a spindle of white cotton thread and a generous supply of Rocaille beads, by the technique of threading. The pleasant turquoise background provides a wonderful contrast for the nine sprays of floral motifs (eight along the circumference and one in the centre) naturalistically depicted in shades of yellow, green and rose-pink. The yellow and green floral border and the fringe of strong yellow beads completed this aesthetically pleasing work of art. Probably late nineteenth/early twentieth century. From Penang. Collection of Mrs Grace Saw.

climate of the tropics, not to mention the host of mites, silverfish, cockroaches and other little vermin, which are particularly destructive to silk, cotton and linen fabrics, it is a matter of some urgency that these highly perishable works of art should be preserved (at least on written records) in a more permanent fashion before they crumble to dust and oblivion.

Although most of the extant pieces are undated, none of them on circumstantial evidence, are perhaps older than eighty or ninety years. Many, when examined under a magnifying glass, are already showing signs of deterioration. Unless something is done to fumigate these artefacts and preserve them in moisture-free, dust-free and insect-proof conditions, there is a real danger that these irreplaceable works of art will be largely lost several decades from now. Museum conservation-

Fig. 5 A pair of necktie-shaped, ornamental hangings, traditionally used for hanging from the front of the four-poster, red-and-gold, Straits Chinese wedding bed. It was the handiwork of Straits nonyas, and shows a combination of fine silk embroidery executed mainly with satin stitches, and threaded bead panels and tassels. Notice the bright and striking colours. Late nineteenth/early twentieth century. From Penang. Collection of Mrs Grace Saw.

ists are also aware that the atmosphere of most industrialized cities nowadays is filled with corrosive and acidic chemicals which have very adverse effects upon fabric materials. This third volume on Straits Chinese Heritage is an attempt to record these artefacts in pictures and in printed words before they deteriorate irreparably and become permanently forgotten.

One other thing which I should like to note here is that anyone who attempts to do scholarly research on beads, bead-making and the role which beads play in the customs and traditions of some culture, whether ancient or modern, is faced with an immediate difficulty, namely, the scarcity of published works on the subject. I am not referring to manuals which provide detailed and interesting instructions on how to string, thread or weave bracelets, necklaces, head-bands or collars, by using Rocaille, stone, metal, wood or even plastic (!) beads. These are easily available in bookshops. But books which set out to describe and explain the role of beads from a historical, cultural and aesthetic point of view are extremely hard to come by.

This is perhaps ironical because beads and their uses have always featured very conspicuously in the cultures of most ancient societies including those of Mesopotamia, Egypt, Persia, Harappa and Mohenjo-Daro, Mexico and those of other Central and South American states[3] where the Maya, Toltec, Aztec and Inca cultures had flourished from remote antiquity up to the fifteenth century A.D. Many tribal societies in Africa, Asia, North America, Polynesia and Melanesia also used beads and beaded ornaments very extensively in their religious and social ceremonies. However, a thorough check through the extensive catalogue of the British Library (formerly the British Museum Library) in London several years ago, elicited only about half a dozen titles on the history of beads and beadwork. There is practically nothing in these few published works about ancient or modern Chinese beads, let alone about the beadwork of that small but unique community of overseas Chinese in Southeast Asia, namely, the peranakans or babas of the former Straits Settlements, and those of Java and Sumatra.

In preparing this essay, therefore, I have had to rely very largely upon the evidence presented by the various samples of beadwork shown in this book and those belonging to private collectors in Singapore, Malaysia and Indonesia. Much of what I have to say about Straits Chinese beadwork here consist of conjectures, inferences and information derived from a study of these artefacts going back to 1970, and of what I have learnt over the years concerning the peculiarities in the customs and traditions of the baba-nonyas of the Straits Settlements era. Since practically no research has been done on the subject, this is perhaps the most rational alternative left. But more fundamentally, no description of any cultural artefact, however detailed or scientifically accurate, is of any significance, unless it is made against a background knowledge of the cultural setting in which the artefact plays a role. For while a work of art can be appreciated either for its technical accomplishment, or perhaps, its aesthetic qualities, it is the cultural matrix from which it springs that most works of art owe much of their fascination.

This book is, therefore, not a practical manual on beadwork and embroidery. The reader will not find descriptions and illustrations on how to execute beadwork of various sorts; nor will he find instructions on how to execute embroidery stitches, what threads, needles and fabrics to use, where to obtain patterns, or how to transfer them to the fabric. There are many fascinating and informative books on the subject. I am mainly concerned with the description and explanation of Straits Chinese beadwork and embroidery from a historical and cultural point of view, because hitherto no published work on the subject has been attempted before.

PART I

STRAITS CHINESE BEADWORK

2
The Romance
of Ancient Beads

BEADS AND BEADED ornaments are usually associated with cheap and inferior glass trinkets which, in the days gone by, were greatly prized by various Red Indian tribes, head-hunters from Borneo and New Guinea, most African tribes, cannibalistic tribes, and other wild and barbarous 'savages' living in remote desert places, inaccessible mountains, or perhaps, some impenetrable jungles in the tropics. For this reason, 'civilized' folk are apt to turn up their noses at the mention of beads and beaded ornaments. Most people are, however, not aware that beaded ornaments made by ancient and primitive people can be of cultural and aesthetic interest.

The prevailing prejudice is that only items of jewellery which command high monetary value, such as gold, platinum and precious stones including diamonds, rubies, sapphires, emeralds and imperial green jades, are worthy of attention and admiration. Hence, beads and beaded ornaments, whether of ancient vintage, or crafted with skill and imagination, are hastily dismissed as worthless baubles of no importance except to people living under primitive conditions.

The purpose of this preamble is to describe very briefly, the role which beads and beaded ornaments play in the history of ancient societies – and the history of beads goes back 6,000 years. What is not often realized concerning ancient beads is that there is more to these humble pieces of glass,

stones, minerals and metals than meets the eye. Associated with beads and beaded ornaments in every culture are facts, legends, superstitions, mystery and romance, no less fascinating than the sheer beauty of beads and beaded ornaments, or the creative imagination which went into their craftsmanship. I shall merely confine myself to some of the more significant facts about beads.

To begin with, the history of beads is probably as old if not older, than that of the written script; and it goes back to the time of the most ancient civilizations of man, namely, Egypt and Mesopotamia. As long ago as the fourth millennium B.C., the Egyptians and the Sumerians learnt, after a considerable period of experimenting, how to make glass beads in imitation of the more expensive types of precious and semi-precious stones, namely, lapis-lazuli, turquoise, carnelian, amber, rock-crystal, amethyst, rubies, jasper, chalcedony, etc. These were known as 'faience beads', a variety of 'baked' beads made out of powdered quartz and limestone.

Faience beads

Since faience beads came to play an important role in the history of the development of beads and beaded ornaments, we shall pause here to describe very briefly, the technique of fabricating these beads. First, the bead-maker prepared a fine paste consisting of powdered quartz or sand and lime-stone. The paste was then fashioned into beads of different shapes (spherical, cylindrical, biconical, ovoidal, disc-like, etc.) and a hollow was pierced into each bead by one or several tiny sticks. These beads were then placed on a slab of earthenware and lowered into a furnace to bake in a low fire. After heating for a short while, the beads were taken out of the furnace and a solution of soda glaze mixed with compounds of copper oxides was applied over the surface of these beads and fired once more. The heat would cause the alkali glaze to adhere to the surface of the beads, while the sticks in the perforations burned away, to produce shiny faience beads.

In predynastic times between, say, 4000 and 3000 B.C., the ancient Egyptians (and the Sumerians as well) had already learnt the art of applying copper alkalis to produce several varieties of blue and blue-green faience beads with a semi-vitreous glaze. But apparently, they were not entirely satisfied with their efforts; for they went on improving upon their techniques in the hope of hitting upon the right sorts of metal or mineral oxides for producing faience beads of many colours and shades.

The idea was to make beads which would have the colours and textures simulating precious and semi-precious stones, especially the magnificent blue of lapis-lazuli; the various shades of green simulating turquoise, jade or malachite; the reds of carnelian, agate, ruby and garnet; the yellow of amber or calcite; and the black of jets. Where their ancient chemists failed to imitate the appearance and texture of precious and semi-precious stones in faience beads, they continued to employ natural minerals for the making of beads. But rock minerals belonging to the family of quartz are extremely hard, and have to be rubbed down by abrasives at considerable labour. That is why excavations of tombs in ancient Egypt and Meso-

potamia dating to this period, still yielded a lot of lapis-lazuli, agate, carnelian, chalcedony and turquoise beads. But by about 1500 B.C. or thereabouts, Egyptian chemists had practically mastered the necessary secrets of making faience beads with blue, blue-green, green, yellow, red, white and lilac glazes.

The quality of Egyptian faience beads was so good that they could have passed off, and had in fact been passed off, as lapis-lazuli, turquoise, carnelian, amber, jasper and chalcedony. Even modern experts were fooled by ancient Egyptian bead-makers. For, according to Cyril Aldred, an expert of Egyptology, 'Some of the objects from the tomb of Tut-ankh-amun have, for instance, been catalogued as inlaid with lapis-lazuli, carnelian and feldspar, *when glass simulating those stones would have been a more accurate description*'.[4] (Italics mine.)

This signal achievement of ancient technology, well-received even by the priestly and aristocratic classes in Egypt (and later all over Africa and the Middle East), is borne out by the fact that some of the finest funeral jewels and ornaments of Tut-ankh-amun were fabricated out of faience beads or inlays of faience enamels.

Although some of the outer chambers of Tut-ankh-amun's tomb, which was discovered by Howard Carter in 1927, were partially plundered by grave-robbers, the burial chamber containing the royal sarcophagus and other belongings of the Pharaoh, was untouched. It was in this chamber that some of the masterpieces of ancient Egyptian jewellers' art were found, including those gorgeous pectorals, necklaces, collar pieces, diadems, belts, bracelets, arm-circlets, earrings and stoles. The Cairo Museum and the Metropolitan Museum in New York own some of the finest collections of Tut-ankh-amun's personal jewels and insignias of office.

As for the Sumerians, and later, the Babylonians, who inhabited the cities scattered in the valleys between the Tigris and Euphrates rivers, they, too, were excellent craftsmen and jewellers. Excavations by Sir Leonard Woolley between 1922 and 1928 in the city of Ur[5] also uncovered faience beads in addition to those made of gold, lapis-lazuli, carnelian, agate and chalcedony. Sumerian beads were of a variety of shapes, including biconical, barrel-shaped, discoidal, spherical beads. The finest grave containing many gold ornaments and faience beads was that belonging to Phabi, Queen of Shubad. A lovely necklace belonging to the Queen was strung with graduated spherical ribbed beads made of gold and grey faience. The Sumerians did not, however, equal the excellence of craftsmanship attained by the Egyptians.

Those who have studied ancient Egyptian jewellery are unanimous in their opinion that those unknown and unnamed glass-makers and jewellers who fabricated the ornaments and personal jewellery of members of the royal and priestly castes down the ages, achieved standards of craftsmanship which remain unsurpassed to this day. For ancient Egyptian beaded ornaments are noted not only for their superb workmanship, but also for their beautiful and original designs, and their splendid colours. And old faience beads, especially the variety having the texture and colours of lapis-lazuli and turquoise, are said to be inimitable even with today's superior technology for making glass-and-enamel products. Experts apparently have little difficulty in distinguishing between old faience beads and modern reproductions: old faience beads are more evenly textured and have a more subtle range of blue and cream-yellow colours.

Several bracelets and necklaces with coronation pectorals found in the funerary chamber of Tut-ankh-amun are replete with blue faience beads and inlays. They are shown on plates 97, 106, 110 and 111 of K. E. Mallakh's and C. Brackman's *The Gold of Tutankhamen*, Newsweek Book, N.Y.

1978, and plates 68, 69, 70, 71 and 72 of Cyril Aldred's *Jewels of the Pharaohs*, Ballantine Books, N.Y., 1978. Perhaps the most impressive inlays of blue faience of ancient Egypt are to be seen in those broad horizontal and vertical stripes in the *nemes* head-dress of the solid gold funerary mask of Tut-ankh-amun.

Thus, while it is true that old beads and beaded ornaments – whether they be of faience inlays or of natural stones – were made in societies which are primitive by modern standards of technology, there was nothing shoddy or 'primitive' about their standard of craftsmanship. In fact, quite the opposite is true; for old beads and beaded ornaments were hand-crafted with such patience and loving care that each one took on a characteristic charm of its own – something that cannot be said of mass-produced articles with their nondescript quality.

There is one other thing which must be said about old beads and beaded ornaments: if one takes some trouble to examine the various circumstances which surrounded the uses of these artefacts, one would soon discover that they have more than mere cosmetic functions in the lives of many people throughout ancient and even certain modern societies.

Beads, when fabricated into necklaces, pendants, collar-pieces, head-dresses, bracelets, sceptres, diadems and coverings for thrones, for example, served as insignias of status, authority and power. The ancient Pharaohs of Egypt wore broad, multi-chained collar pieces, beaded diadems, necklaces and pectorals as symbols of their supreme power and authority. The nobility and priestly caste also wore an incredible variety of beaded ornaments on state functions and ceremonies.

Among the Pueblo Indians of North America, necklaces of jades were worn only by their chiefs. The kings of the Aztecs and the Mayas wore beaded jade necklaces and jade masks. Beaded objects had social and political significance in certain African societies; among the Bang-wa tribes and the Cameronian tribes, the natives fashioned wooden stools or chairs and clothed them with beaded suits. Beaded stools were jealously guarded symbols of royal power.

The ancient kings of Benin in West Africa known as Oba, regularly wore suits, multi-chained necklaces and head-dresses made entirely out of tubular red coral beads as emblems of royal power. Their queens wore multi-chained chokers and high-pointed head-dresses also made out of tubular, red coral beads. Such beaded coral ornaments were the exclusive prerogatives of Benin royalty.

Examples of beads and beaded ornaments employed as symbols of royal status, ecclesiastical power and tribal solidarity can be multiplied indefinitely, but one more example of the role played by beads in the lives of people will suffice. From a very early period in the history of Christianity, beads strung together to form a rosary were intended for devotees in counting prayers; the English word 'bead' is in fact derived from a Middle English word 'bede', which is related to a Saxon word 'biddan', and which is in turn derived from a Teutonic word of a similar spelling meaning 'to pray'. The word 'prayer' and 'bead' are therefore etymologically related.

Thus, far from being cheap and inferior glass trinkets used only by cannibals, head-hunters and other 'savages' for their 'diabolical' ceremonies, beads and beaded ornaments were, from the earliest civilizations of man, used by royalty, nobility and the priestly caste as symbols of power, authority, wealth and divine origin. Not all beads are 'cheap and worthless glass trinkets'; some were made of gold and silver, while others were fabricated out of lapis-lazuli, green jadeite, agate, jasper, carnelian, garnet, turquoise, chalcedony, corals, pearls and other precious and semi-precious stones.

And as for glass beads, the blue and blue-green faience beads made by the Egyptians and the Phoenicians, these were highly valued even in ancient times among the nations of the Middle East, Africa, Asia and Europe. Faience beads were used as a currency not only for the exchange of goods and services, but also as payment of tributes. The ancient Egyptians and Phoenicians regularly included faience beads in their inventory of goods to be bartered with the various tribes in the interior of Africa, and for a very long time (several thousand years in fact) blue and blue-green faience beads were greatly sought after and readily accepted by most people.

During the Roman Empire, in the reigns of Octavian and Augustus, the Imperial Roman Government accepted old Egyptian faience as tributes from vassal states and dependencies, including Egypt herself. The tribal chiefs of many African states vied with one another for the possession of faience beads from the Pharaonic era, and oftentimes they were prepared to pay for these 'glass trinkets' with gold-dust and gold nuggets. For them, old faience from ancient graves were invested with magical powers. They did not mind even if the beads were worn, faded and pitted, for these were signs of genuine antiquity.

In time, faience beads travelled to India, Burma, Sumatra, Malaya, Indonesia, Borneo and the Oceania.[6] But not all old faience were of Egyptian origin; the Syrians, the Iranians, the Iraqis and even the Indians learnt how to make faience in imitation of their Egyptian variety, and these when exported to Asia became known as 'trade-wind' beads, because the sailing ships which carried them thither followed the paths of the Trade Winds.

3
Straits Chinese Beadwork as a Distinctive Handicraft

WE PASS ON to consider a category of nineteenth century beadwork, namely Straits Chinese beadwork, whose function was purely ornamental. I should state at the outset, therefore, that when we refer to Straits Chinese beadwork in this volume, we are not referring to any of those distinctive types of beads described in the previous chapter – faience, chalcedony, jasper, turquoise, lapis-lazuli, jade, gold, etc., and which were once widely used by peoples of various ancient civilizations. Items made from these beads, like splendid necklaces, disc-shape collars, bracelets, arm-circlets, belts, anklets, diadems, earrings and finger-rings, are not to be found among extant collections of Straits Chinese beadwork.

Straits Chinese beaded ornaments are rarely, if ever, fabricated out of beads with quaint and exotic shapes, such as chevron, pentagon, spot-eye, disc-shaped, banded, diamond-shaped, discoidal, biconical, barrel-shaped, ribbed, and fluted beads. The Straits Chinese never seemed to have acquired a taste for old faience beads, for such beads have never been found among their family heirlooms. They showed no interest in beads made out of turquoise, coral, lapis-lazuli or agate, partly because these artefacts struck them as primitive and barbarous, and partly because beads and beaded *ornaments* did not play an important role in Chinese culture. The ancient Emperors and Empresses of China did, of course, use jade beads

in their personal ornaments, but they were never decked with a profusion of beaded ornaments like the Pharaohs of Egypt or the Chiefs of various African tribes.

Beads of such ancient vintage are conspicuously absent in Straits Chinese culture because, unlike tribal people, particularly their chiefs and their witch-doctors, the baba-nonyas of Singapore, Malacca and Penang did not use beads and beaded ornaments either as status symbols to indicate social and financial standing, or even as personal ornaments. To adorn themselves, the womenfolk especially preferred gold, silver, platinum, diamonds, rubies, sapphires, emeralds and other precious and semi-precious stones which have been fashioned by skilled jewellers into items of magnificent jewellery. Indeed, necklaces, earrings, bracelets, arm-circlets and diadems which have been fabricated out of large and curiously made beads of the types used in ancient times never acquired that aura of prestige with the sophisticated and urbanized nonyas. They did not want to be decked like Orang Asli or tribal women.

For the baba-nonyas, neither beads nor beaded ornaments were invested with magical or superstitious properties: they attached no religious, spiritual or symbolic significance to beaded artefacts. For this reason, they did not attempt to make ancestral idols and nature spirits and clothe with beaded suits and beaded ornaments, as certain African tribes were fond of doing. They have no

Fig. 6 Among the quaint and exotic fineries of the traditional Straits Chinese bridal chamber must be included this pair of handsome hexagonal vases. Each vase was fabricated out of six panels of stitched beads sewn together at the sides. Height including wooden stand: 8 inches. From Penang. Collection of Mrs Grace Saw.

Fig. 7 A pair of butterfly ornaments executed entirely with stitched beads on both the obverse and reverse sides. Butterflies, in ancient China, symbolized conjugal fidelity and were thus always associated with weddings. Greatest width: 6 inches. From Penang. Collection of Mrs Grace Saw.

fetishes made out of beads, and as far as I know, beaded ornaments play no significant role in their funeral ceremonies either.

Although the nonyas were noted for their love of ostentation, their items of jewellery definitely did not include beaded ornaments. It was quite unthinkable for them to adorn themselves with fanciful and colourful ornaments made out of beads and feathers after the fashion of many tribes in Africa, Polynesia and Micronesia. Except for the pair of beaded slippers which every traditional nonya wore at home and out-of-doors, beaded jewellery is conspicuously absent in her personal attire.

The only time beads and beaded ornaments were seen in great profusion – especially in the homes of old Penang baba families – was during the twelve days of elaborate ceremonies and festivities organized to mark a traditional Straits Chinese wedding. Keen-eyed observers would notice an astonishing variety of beaded and beaded-cum-embroidered ornaments carefully laid out in the bridal chamber, lending an air of festive splendour and ostentation to this auspicious occasion.

Among these items would be conspicuous rectangular silk embroidered panels enhanced with trimmings of beaded borders and beaded tassels made to fit the lintels of doors and windows in the

Fig. 8 This unusual T-shaped ornament, consisting of a narrow, rectangular, silk embroidered panel, with a beaded panel executed entirely by threading and long tassels, was a covering for the red-and-gold bridal dressing mirror. It seemed to have been used exclusively in Straits Chinese homes in Penang. But I have found similar panels, though few and far between, in Malacca. The length of this ornamental covering from top to bottom varies between 19 inches and 21 inches. Collection of Mrs Grace Saw.

bridal chamber and the carved frontal beam of the four-poster wedding bed; beaded and embroidered pillow cases; beaded panels for small tea-tables; bed-runners of threaded or stitched beads meant for the front side of the mattress; beaded panels (usually circular) for the top of food covers; beaded and beaded-cum-embroidered slippers and shoes for the bride and groom and wedding guests; belts; collar and shoulder pieces; the brims of ceremonial mandarin hats; spectacle cases; wallets and purses; comb-boxes; decorative panels of wedding foot-stools; pillow and bolster ends; and other gewgaws, some of which are curiously fashioned after the shapes of peaches, star fruits, finger citrons, butterflies, bats, fishes, symbols of scholarly accomplishments, etc. Such curiosities (see fig. 7) are fashioned three-dimensionally and painstakingly stitched with thousands of tiny coloured glass beads.

These splendid ornaments, fabricated entirely out of small Rocaille beads, were individually handcrafted by the nonyas themselves. Many long and dreary months of patient work went into the stringing, stitching and threading of these artefacts (see figs. 8 & 9). Unlike embroidered panels and ornamental articles which could be purchased ready-made from local embroidery shops, the travelling haberdasher or embroidery dealers in

Fig. 9 One of a pair of wedding stools with an ogival beaded panel serving as a sort of cushion cover. Bridal stools with beaded covers are very rarely seen nowadays, though they must have been fairly common in the heirlooms of well-to-do Straits Chinese homes in Malacca, Penang and Singapore in the days gone by. A similar pair of wedding stools acquired in Malacca many years ago is in Mrs Ho Wing Meng's collection. Property of Mr Peter Wee.

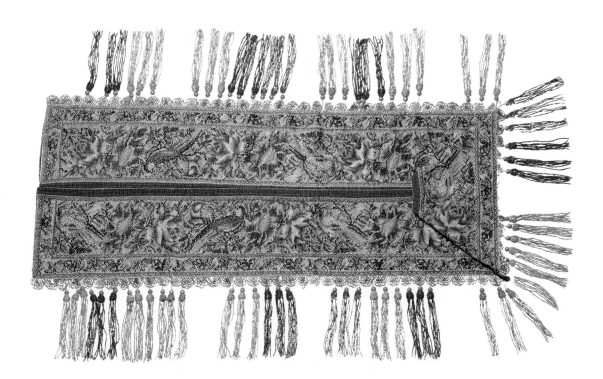

Fig. 10 This long narrow panel of closely threaded Rocaille beads with tassels, over five feet long, was originally intended to be attached to the bottom of one of those long silk embroidered panels either meant for the wedding bed, or else for the lintel of the door to the bridal chamber. Because Rocaille beads used by the Straits nonyas were between 0.75 and 1 mm, the fabrication of one of these panels by the method of threading, required several hundred thousand beads! Collection of Mrs Grace Saw.

Fig. 11 Ornamental beaded panels for covering either the dressing mirror or the mirror on the carved, red-and-gold wash-stand. The main beaded panel with blue-green ground and red and yellow peony blossoms is executed entirely by threading, while the exceptionally long tassel work is done by stringing of Rocaille beads. The unusual feature is the topmost panel of golden velvet appliquéd with ten religious figures of silvergilt. The art of threading beads seems to have been lost to the surviving generation of nonyas today. Collection of Mrs Grace Saw.

Canton or Shanghai, beadwork of the type shown here had to be fabricated at home. They could not be procured at local haberdasheries or bought directly from embroidery dealers in China, because cottage industries dedicated to the making of beadwork were practically non-existent. The Chinese never seemed to have developed a tradition of beadwork comparable to the quality, the variety and ingenuity of workmanship distinguishing those of ancient Egypt or the tribal nations of Africa. And among the various communities of immigrant Chinese in Malaya, only the Straits Chinese, following Malay customs and traditions, took to the art of making beaded ornaments for their wedding ceremonies. The more conservative Chinese communities, however, showed no interest in this local tradition, regarding it barbarous and alien to the mainstream of Chinese civilization.

Of course, the Straits Chinese, like their more conservative compatriots, also used embroidered articles and apparel made to their specifications very lavishly, for their wedding ceremonies. Their womenfolk, as we shall see in Part II, also embroidered smaller articles with their own hands. However, the larger embroidered articles (some with trimmings of beaded panels made locally) were largely imported from Canton and Shanghai. These were ordered directly or purchased through local embroidery shops which kept adequate stocks of drapes, bed-covers, banners, valances, robes, panels, etc., to meet the requirements of merchants, traders, householders, clans, associations, temples, business houses and funeral parlours. But whereas the more conservative Chinese communities were content to wear and display embroidered articles on important festive occasions, the Straits Chinese made it their custom to include gorgeous ornaments of beadwork among their items of embroidered finery.

What evidence do we have that these articles of beadwork were the products of a bygone generation of nonyas who flourished during the nineteenth and early twentieth century? Apart from the avowals of the older nonyas still alive today, there are still a few among them who can stitch the ornamental covers of a pair of typical nonya slippers, small beaded panels and other articles of virtu. The stringing of small Rocaille beads is, of course, relatively easy, and proficiency in manipulating threads and needles for stringing beads can be acquired within a short time. But the art of *threading* beads to create panels of intricate patterns is practically non-existent today.

I have met many old nonyas during the last fifteen years, but none seemed to have professed the knowledge of threading beads for creating complex panels of the ones shown in figs. 1, 8, 10 & 11. However, the fact that practically no old nonyas today seem to know how to execute the complex threading procedures for producing intricate panels of this type, does not mean that these extant pieces of beaded panels could not have been made by their predecessors in the days gone by. Not at all. If anything, it simply means that the art of threading beads went out of fashion with the passing away of a former generation of skilled and patient nonyas. Besides, we have here before us, these articles which were ferreted out of disused camphor-wood trunks in old Straits Chinese homes, and which, by general consensus of present-day baba-nonyas, were attributed to the handiwork of their predecessors. From a stylistic point of view, the unique patterns on these beaded panels could only have been conceived by artisans who were intimately familiar with baba tastes.

Since such beaded ornaments do not occur among the trappings and finery of a traditional Chinese wedding in China, it is evident that the traditional Straits Chinese custom of using and displaying beaded panels and beaded ornaments of ingenious and complex craftsmanship in their wedding ceremonies was largely derived from the customs of Minangkabau Malays in Malacca, Negri

Fig. 12 This impressive segment of a larger embroidered panel has all its decorative designs executed in couched gold threads. The exclusive application of formalized and foliated designs indicate that it is a product of Malay workmanship. Dimensions: 18 by 10 inches including beaded tassels. Probably late nineteenth century. From Malacca. Author's collection.

Sembilan and Johore (see fig. 12).

As has already been noted by some historians, and according to oral traditions of the babas, many of the early Chinese who first came to trade and settle in Malacca at the beginning of the Ming dynasty during the fourteenth century, adopted the practice of marrying non-Muslim Malay, Javanese or Balinese girls, so that their native spouses could help to maintain their shops, whenever they were away on trading missions.[7] This intermarriage between early Chinese traders and native girls of local or regional origin produced, in time, a community of Malayanised Chinese whose culture showed a curious mixture of ancient Chinese and Hindu-Islamic influences –

clearly manifested in Straits Chinese culture. And the evidence (as I have shown elsewhere)[8] that the Straits Chinese culture was greatly influenced by the customs, beliefs and practices of Islamic Malay, and to a certain extent, Hindu origins (of the cultures of the Srivijaya and the Majapahit era) is easily adduced. This would include their peculiar Malay patois, namely, Baba Malay, which consists largely of words derived from Malay and the Hokkien dialect, their special nonya cuisine incorporating mainly local Malay ingredients and techniques of cooking, the traditional nonya attire, their dances and *pantun* recitation, and certain aspects of their wedding customs and religious practices incorporating a mixture of Confucianism,

Buddhism, Taoism and Malay animism. But more particularly, if we take the trouble to examine the various kinds of ceremonial artefacts which the local Malays, especially those of Minangkabau origin, used for their weddings, we soon discover that beadwork very similar to the types discussed here, also featured prominently among the various paraphernalia of the bridal trousseau.[9]

Thus, apart from the kinds of beads employed (i.e. seed beads of the variety known as 'Rocaille glass beads'), the shapes as well as the ceremonial functions of old Malay beadwork, parallel those found in Straits Chinese homes. Likewise, the standard of workmanship is as good, if not better, as the best of Straits Chinese craftsmanship. The only significant difference is in the kinds of motifs employed in the decorative designs of these artefacts.

Whereas the Malays, conforming to Koranic injunctions against idolatry, employed exclusively conventionalized floral, arabesque and geometric motifs for all their designs, the Straits Chinese subscribed to a curious mixture of Confucian, Buddhist and Taoist beliefs, and were of a more liberal cast of mind. They were thus free to select their decorative motifs from a vast and varied repertoire of auspicious and religious symbols inherent in Chinese art – and Islamic art as well.

Since Straits Chinese beaded ornaments were exclusively intended for wedding ceremonies, the decorative symbols employed had to be restricted to those which were representative of conjugal happiness, fidelity, fertility, prosperity, harmony, scholarly achievement and longevity. These include bats, a pair of fishes and a pair of magpies (symbols of conjugal happiness), a pair of butterflies and a pair of mandarin ducks (for conjugal fidelity), bamboos (for strength and resilience), a pair of cranes, peaches and stags (symbols of longevity), pomegranates (for fertility), peonies (for springtime – an auspicious time to get married), and of course, a pair of phoenixes representing the wedded couple.

It should be clear by now that Straits Chinese beadwork is culturally and stylistically different from all other types of extant beaded ornaments, and that, among Straits Chinese cultural artefacts, beadwork is the only category which was authentically produced by the nonyas. However, it owes its form and functions to old Hindu-Malay customs and practices, its decorative designs to ancient Chinese art motifs and the various beliefs associated with the uses of these motifs, and its techniques of craftsmanship to Malay and other cultures of ancient vintage.

Nonetheless, like all things typical of Straits Chinese culture, it is not a slavish imitation of the various cultures from which it originally drew its inspiration. Instead, the traditional Straits Chinese borrowed only those features of foreign cultures which were essential to their needs, while modifying other aspects to make them conform to peculiar customs and beliefs. The resultant culture which eventually emerged was unique to their community (see fig. 13).

For this reason, Straits Chinese beadwork is like that of no other culture, whether ancient or extant, and it is therefore unlikely to be encountered outside the various Straits Chinese communities in Penang, Malacca, Singapore and Indonesia, as several collectors have noted in their discussions with me. Most extant beadwork, apart from those found in old homes, are in private collections. Collectors of Malayana recognized the artistic qualities of these artefacts and their cultural significance at least a decade before the museum authorities of Malaysia and Singapore decided that they should be included in our cultural heritage. The National Museum of Singapore, the Muzium Negara of Kuala Lumpur, the Malacca State Museum and the Penang State Museum now have permanent exhibits of antique Straits Chinese artefacts, including Straits Chinese beadwork.

Fig. 13 The two circular ornaments with designs of embroidered Rocaille beads, unless carefully scrutinized, could easily pass off as beaded table-mats of British handiwork made during the Victorian era. For one thing, the beads are either of British or French make. But the moment one looks closely at the designs, it becomes apparent that motifs such as phoenixes, finger citrons, peonies, cocks and quails are obviously of foreign or European aesthetic designs. This *mélange* of different cultures is another characteristic of the *objets d'arts* peculiar to the Straits Chinese. Diameter: 8 inches. Probably late nineteenth/early twentieth century. From Penang. Collection of Mrs Grace Saw.

4
Beads, Threads and Needles

THE BEADS USED in Straits Chinese bead-work are seed beads, a variety of eighteenth/nineteenth century trade-wind beads. Trade-wind glass beads of a somewhat larger variety, between 2 and 3 mm in size, were largely used during the eighteenth century and throughout the nineteenth century by European traders for bartering with the native tribes of Asia, Africa, North America, Polynesia and Micronesia.

The term 'seed beads' refers to beads of whatever materials, be they seeds of fruits, tiny seashells, pearls, minerals, metals or glass beads as long as they are small like seeds. The smallest I have seen so far are about 0.5 mm across, and the largest used in Straits Chinese beaded ornaments are about 5 mm in size. Occasionally one encounters beads as big as 10 mm in diameter, but these were employed very sparingly as finials or terminating decorations of some sort, never in necklaces, bracelets, ear-rings, finger-rings or diadems meant for the nonyas.

The other technical name given to seed beads, especially those made of coloured glass, is 'Rocaille beads'. The term 'Rocaille' is a French word which came into common usage during the sixteenth century, when it was specifically used to refer to the kind of rockwork or rockery found in a French garden, *jardin de rocaille*. By the early eighteenth century, 'rocaille' came to be applied to ornaments which resembled French rockeries in their brilliant and showy appearance. Rocaille beads are so called, because ornamental objects made out of such glass beads give off a similar colourful and scintillating effect.

The best of Rocaille beads are spheroidal (compressed at the sides) rather than round, and the types traditionally preferred by former generations of Straits nonyas, were no bigger than 0.5 mm in size. Beads are classified from '1' to '10', that is, from the largest to the smallest. Hence, the bigger the code number, the smaller the size of the bead. The majority of extant antique beadwork are, however, stitched, strung or threaded with Rocaille beads between, say, 0.75 and 1 mm. But even so, these beads are considerably smaller than those types commonly used by native tribes in Africa, Asia (particularly Southeast Asia), Micronesia, Polynesia and North America. Trade-wind beads of this type may be up to 2 mm in diameter.

Straits nonyas also used another variety of Rocaille beads, between 1 and 1.5 mm long and cylindrical in shape. These beads are glassy and brilliantly coloured. They appeared to have been produced in large quantities in Birmingham, England, and possibly Geneva, and Venice in Italy. The best of Rocaille beads, however, have a quiet luminosity and pearly opalescence about

Fig. 14 Rocaille beads of the type prized by the traditional Straits nonyas were apparently never sold in bulk quantities, which the term 'pound beads' seems to suggest. As shown here, the finer of Rocaille beads were always sold in small bundles strung together by cotton threads between 6 and 8 cm long. The topmost group of beads consists of small metal beads about 0.5 mm in diameter. The group of beads on the left consists of spheroidal glass beads, while tubular beads, about 1.25 mm in length, have been grouped on the right. Collection of Mrs Ho Wing Meng.

them, and they were mostly made in Lyons in the south of France.

In their terminology of beads, the traditional nonyas used virtually one term to describe the various beads they employed in their beadwork, namely, *manek potong* (literally, 'cut beads'). Technically speaking, most extant types of glass beads are cut beads, in the sense that the raw beads used in a bead factory consist of bits and pieces of thin, hollow glass-tubings. But in the finished products, beads emerge in a variety of shapes, such as spheroidal, ellipsoidal, biconical, squarish, round and cylindrical. The term *manek potong*, while technically correct, does not distinguish between the various types of beads.

Rocaille beads of the varieties used in Straits Chinese beadwork are among the smallest of seed beads; generally they are transparent without appearing glassy and garish, because there is an even and subdued glow about their colours. This quiet but luminescent quality is not found among the larger variety of beads used by the various native tribes in other parts of the world. The finest type of Rocaille beads range from between 0.5 and 0.6 mm in diameter for the smallest beads, and those which are almost 1 mm in size.

A variety of Rocaille beads, known as 'Rotelle' beads, is made of similar material, namely, glass, and cut in similar flattened spherical shape. However, Rotelle beads have bigger holes. The fact that mainly Rocaille beads of between size 10 and size 8 (i.e. between 0.5 mm and about 1 mm in diameter) are widely used in the making of Straits Chinese beadwork is significant. These beaded ornaments have a finer texture and feel about them, which is no doubt attributable to a combination of several factors, namely, the diminutive sizes of the beads employed, the shimmering glow of their colours and the complex subtleties of their designs. The overall effect is a sensation of pleasant colours and refined craftsmanship. By contrast, most tribal beadwork, which combines a larger and coarser variety of trade-wind beads in flat and opaque colours with their characteristically bold and geometric designs, tends to give an overall impression of barbarous splendour, especially those huge, stiff collar discs of colourful beads worn by the Masai tribes of Africa.

The finest beads used in Straits Chinese beadwork are metal beads (also of French origin) covered with tiny diamond facetings and no bigger than 0.5 mm in size. Because of their faceted surfaces, these beads have a built-in glitter about them. They were less frequently used, and must have cost more than glass beads.

Rocaille beads are usually strung in little bundles of white cotton threads, each bundle consisting of ten short strands of strung beads (see fig. 14). The length of each strand varies between 6 and 8 cm, while the number of beads per strand depends upon the length of the thread and the size of the beads. For example, if each strand is 8 cm long, and each bead is 0.5 mm in diameter, there should be 160 beads in each strand and 1,600 beads per bundle of 10 strands of beads. Sometimes the beads are tied together in sets of 10 bundles instead of separately in one bundle. Beads sold in small bundles were more costly, and French Rocaille and metal beads – the types favoured by the nonyas – were more expensive than the larger variety of tubular glass beads with a coarser texture and a more glassy appearance.

Although trade-wind glass beads of the type used by European traders for bartering with the native tribes of Africa, Asia and Oceania during the eighteenth and nineteenth century were sold by the pounds, thus the name 'pound beads', fine Rocaille beads of the types favoured by the nonyas were rarely, if ever, sold by the pounds. As far as I can remember, Rocaille beads sold by the Chinese haberdasher were never weighed on small brass-and-ivory scales, but were sold in little bundles tied together with cotton threads.

Nowadays only the older generation of Singaporeans can recall the travelling Chinese haberdasher, or jarong, who went from house to house hawking his collection of fascinating articles by twirling a circular rattle back and forth in his hand to produce the characteristic 'tok-tok-tok . . . tok-tok-tok . . .' sound which could be heard at least a couple of hundred yards down the road. He now belongs to the breed of itinerant traders who disappeared from the streets of Singapore at least forty years ago.

I remember well that my mother and aunts used to purchase all their supplies of colourful silk and cotton threads, balls of woollen threads for knitting, needles, tapes, laces, cotton gauze, buttons, beads, sequins, velvets and tambour frames of various sizes from the jarong-man, who always went about peddling his three-wheeled vehicle. He usually wore a blue or black silk garment consisting of a loose, long-sleeved tunic with silken fasteners and a pair of baggy pants (babas referred to this costume as baju loksuan). Over his head, he wore a broad-brimmed, peasant hat which spread beyond his shoulders to protect him from the fierce heat of the tropics. His feet were shod with black velvet shoes. And whenever mother needed a fresh supply of threads, needles, buttons and beads, she would tell us to hail the jarong-man, and one of us would rush out into the street, yelling 'Jarong!' at the top of his voice several times. He would invariably arrive a few minutes later, eager to show

Fig. 15 Six boxes of brilliantly coloured, French sequins (the labels identify their provenance as Lyons in the south of France) of various fascinating shapes. The largest of these sequins are 8 mm long, while the smallest ones are 3 mm long. Although they are reputed to be at least seventy years old, the colours show no signs of deterioration in the damp and humid climate of the tropics – a fact which confirms the long-held belief that French Rocaille beads and their accessories were of superior quality. Such sequins were used in combination with Rocaille and metal beads, and even gold and silver threads, for embellishing the designs of Straits Chinese beadwork and embroidery. Collection of Mrs Ho Wing Meng.

us his range of goods.

Inside each of those little drawers built into the front and sides of a big wooden cabinet mounted on his tricycle he carried a fascinating assortment of colourful things. There were boxes upon boxes of buttons of every shape, colour and design; twirls of silk threads with their characteristic sheen and brilliant colours; cotton threads of different weaves and colours; balls of thick woollen threads; piles of delicate white laces with intricate designs; sheets of velvets of deep colours and fine texture; needles of all sizes; Chinese cloth buttons or fasteners of beautiful designs; beads and sequins of incredible beauty; and so on. The *jarong*-man always attracted a small crowd of wide-eyed children who came to gasp at the beautiful things he sold to their mothers.

The colours of old Rocaille beads, especially those of French make, are extremely durable. The shimmering and opalescent enamels which were infused, coated, layered or stippled into the structure of the molten glass rods remained stable and unaffected by the passage of time or the vicissitudes of weather and climate. So it was that collections of old beads recovered from disused camphor chests or needle-boxes left behind by former generations of nonyas, and which may be up to a century old, still preserve their pristine state of freshness and glitter. Since Rocaille beads show little evidence of ageing, it is practically impossible to date a piece of Straits Chinese beadwork by merely examining the condition of the beads. Indications of age are usually elicited from such things as frayed edges on the velvet, cotton or flannel backing, worn-out patches of velvet fibres, worm-holes, missing beads, yellowing of the white cotton threads and stained marks. Datings are therefore arrived at largely through circumstantial evidence, of which the names of the original owners provide a useful clue.

One other variety of beads traditionally used in nonya beadwork must be mentioned here: these are tiny faceted metal beads probably made of brass, no bigger than 0.5 mm in size. They are coated by metal or mineral oxides of various types, and the colours tend to be somewhat sombre. But because these beads are faceted, they give out a dull old glow which seems to have remained unchanged through the years. There is no evidence of chemical decay either. They come in small bundles with each strand of thread carrying about 160 beads or 1,600 beads per bundle of 10 strands of beads. Such beads were used exclusively or in combination with Rocaille beads for stitching and threading, and some of the finest examples of nonya beadwork were constructed out of metal beads alone (see fig. 33).

When working on beaded ornaments, the womenfolk usually had, besides their needle-box containing a varied assortment of needles, threads, little scissors, markers and pieces of cotton fabric, another box filled with bundles of intact Rocaille beads and a collection of small metal containers or plain white porcelain dishes, each of which is filled with beads of one colour only (see fig. 16). These little bead-containers are laid out on the floor (the nonyas always sat on the floor when working with beads or embroidery) to facilitate the stringing, stitching or threading processes. If the work requires stitching of beads, then a *pidangan* or embroidery frame (see pages 51–54 for description) is employed. But stringing and threading required only a needle and some lengths of threads, in addition to the beads.

The manufacture of glass

I shall, for the sake of completeness, give a brief account of the technique of making glass beads, especially of Rocaille beads. But first, a few words about the properties of glass. Glass, as we know it today, is an amalgam produced by heating three principal compounds, namely, silica (in the form of river or seashore sand or pure quartz), calcium oxide (CaO) in the form of limestone or calcium carbonate, and alkaline fluxes consisting mainly of sodium oxide (Na_2O) or soda, and potassium oxide (K_2O) or potash.

Alkaline fluxes are important for facilitating the fusion of the various minerals and for making molten glass highly malleable. Silica is used in the proportion of between 70 and 75 per cent, while calcium oxide (lime), added to give glass its properties of chemical stability and brilliance, consists of about 10 per cent, and the soda or potash fluxes make up the remaining 15 per cent of the chemical composition of glass.

Of course, it is quite possible to vary the composition of the fluxes to make different types of glass: for example, soda glass (i.e. glass in which the principal fluxing agent is sodium oxide) is relatively easy to melt, very highly malleable and

Fig. 16a Here we have a close-up of five dishes containing three varieties of Rocaille beads – blue tubular beads (upper right), 'fish-roe' beads of red, yellow, blue and pink (bottom right) and pearly white and brown beads (bottom left), and one type of metal beads. The dish on the upper left contains small, faceted metallic beads of yellow and saffron colours. Probably of late nineteenth/early twentieth century. Collection of Mrs Ho Wing Meng.

Fig. 16 When working with Rocaille beads, it was customary for the nonyas to have them sorted out into small, shallow metal or porcelain containers: beads of different colours, shapes and sizes are laid out into separate dishes to facilitate the process of stitching, threading or stringing. Collection of Mrs Ho Wing Meng.

thus more easy to manipulate into a variety of shapes and forms.

Glass beads are generally made out of soda glass. Potash glass, on the other hand, has potassium oxide as its principal fluxing agent; it is harder to fuse, very brittle, brilliant, and very much less malleable than soda glass.

There is yet a third type of glass known as 'lead-crystal glass' which was discovered by an Englishman, George Ravenscroft in 1675. Ravenscroft added lead oxide (Pb_2O) to a mixture of silica and potash and produced a heavier but softer glass which gave higher refractive brilliance and 'fire'. Cut glass as we know it today, is potash glass with added lead oxide.[10]

Now in the manufacture of glass, all the three principal mineral and chemical components must be thoroughly mixed in large earthenware crucibles which can withstand high temperatures required for melting silicate crystals. The crucibles containing these mineral and chemical compounds are then fired in furnaces at temperatures in excess of 1000°C until the mixture turns into red-hot, molten glass.

Where the manufacturing processes are intended for the making of coloured glassware, the glass-maker would have to prepare colouring agents in the form of mineral and metal oxides and add them to the mixture of silica, lime and fluxing agents before firing in the furnace.

The colour desired in the final product is determined by the kind of mineral or metal oxides employed before or during fusion. For example, manganese oxide makes glass look yellow, brown, or even violet and purple; chromium oxide gives a grass-green colour; uranium oxide makes the glass look yellowish-green, while antimony and sodium sulphide produce a brilliant yellow colour. Cobalt oxide gives a brilliant blue, while nickel oxide produces a violet blue. Colloidal silver makes glass take on a copper ruby red, while colloidal gold gives a golden ruby red. Bone-glass is made by adding bone-ashes, and opal glass can be achieved by the use of bone-ashes plus feldspar. And so on.

In its molten state, glass is so highly malleable that it can be worked into an extraordinary variety of shapes in the hands of a skilled glass-maker. Certain types of glass objects which require heating, annealing and fast manipulation are usually made close to the furnace sites. But those which require cutting, stippling, engraving or sand-blasting are executed in factories away from the furnace sites.

Molten glass is as malleable if not more so than potter's clay, but even when it has solidified into a rigid, vitreous and transparent substance, it can still be processed and decorated to produce an incredible variety of objects. Thus, depending on whether glass is in its molten or solidified vitreous state, it can be rolled, drawn, pressed, scratched, etched, engraved, stippled, twisted, layered, blown, moulded, stained and even painted upon.

Glass can be made as transparent as clear air, and it can be made so opaque that light cannot pass through. It can be coloured, faceted and shaped to look like jewels. It can be made shatter-proof, heat-proof, corrosion-proof and bullet-proof. And while extant pieces of antique glass objects show various signs of corrosion and decay, it can be made so resistant that it will last indefinitely.

Glass is probably the oldest manufactured product if we go by the glass beads and amulets excavated in Upper Egypt and Mesopotamia. These beads dated to the fourth millennium B.C. are 6,000 years old, and still remarkably preserved.

Rocaille beads

Rocaille beads, strictly speaking, are a variety of glass beads known as 'Drawn beads' because of the curious processes involved. First, the bead-maker must prepare his raw materials by mixing between 70 and 75 per cent by weight of silica with about 10 per cent or more of calcium oxide and about 15 per cent of sodium oxide as a fluxing agent, and the desired quantity of mineral or metal oxide as a colouring agent, in the earthenware crucible. The entire content will then be fired in the furnace till it reaches a red-hot molten state.

The crucible is then taken out of the furnace and stirred thoroughly with a solid iron bar, three or four feet in length. With the tip of this iron bar the bead-maker now draws out a lump of molten glass. Next, he takes a blowpipe (which is nothing more than a hollowed-out iron bar covered with wooden tubing) with another hand, inserts one end to the lump of molten glass, and blows into it to create an air-bubble. By manipulating the two iron rods, he works the bubble of molten glass into a funnel shape.

At this stage (and it must be remembered that working with molten glass requires rapid manipulation, though soda glass solidifies at a slower rate) another worker comes along, grasps the hollowed-out iron rod and walks rapidly, or runs, away from the first worker, and in so doing, pulls the molten lump of glass into a very thin and long hollow tubing of shiny coloured glass which solidifies as it touches the ground.

The faster the second bead-maker walks or runs away by pulling at the molten lump of glass, the thinner is the glass-tubing thus formed. In some instances, it is possible to draw out a very thin glass rod up to 100 metres long. These fine glass rods are then cut into manageable lengths of about one metre, after which they are finely cut into little cylindrical tubings barely 3 to 5 mm in length.

But these little beads are still too sharp at the corners and too uneven in size to be used. They have to be polished smooth and rounded at the edges to give them a somewhat more uniform and spheroid shape. Traditionally, this is done by pouring the entire content of rough-cut beads into a revolving drum containing quartz sand, which is rotated continuously for several hours until the desired roundness and smoothness has been effected.

A variation of this technique requires two workers, each holding a thin, iron blowpipe three to four feet long, to use the tips of their rods to scoop up a small lump of molten glass and blow it into a hollow bulb of glass. Each man then cuts open one end of their hollow molten glass bulb and joins the two bulbs into one.

Having done that, one man will walk away very rapidly from the other person who remains stationary, and in so doing, draws out the glass bulb into a thin tubing of very great length. When the thin glass tubing solidifies, it is cut into shorter tubings, and finally into little tubular beads. These tubular beads are then put into a rotating drum and polished until the beads attain the typical oblate shape.

Because of the minuscule sizes (i.e. 0.5 mm to 1 mm in thickness) and the method of polishing the beads in bulk quantities in rotating spherical drums, Rocaille beads are not all of uniform thickness. Nor are all the beads polished to the same and unvarying standard of roundness and smoothness. Quite to the contrary, it is estimated that at least 5 per cent of the finished beads which emerge from these polishing drums have tiny facetings caused by the accidental effects of the polishing.

Now in normal circumstances, such faceted beads ought to be rejected as spoilt beads. But since Rocaille beads were usually sold in bulk quantities to wholesale dealers, nobody took the trouble to sort out the rejects, as it would have involved a lot of tedious labour. Neither did the Straits nonyas bother to eliminate such 'defective' beads while stitching, stringing or threading beaded panels, even though they must have noticed that there was something unusual about them.

It is just as well that the nonyas did not throw away the faceted beads, because the random scattering of these roughly polished beads on the surface of a typical piece of Straits Chinese beadwork, actually gives it that characteristic glitter and sparkle which would not be there if these 'spoilt' beads had been eliminated in the initial stages of the work. Thus, an accident of manufacture has, in retrospect, become a thing of beauty.

In any case, the rotating or tumbling movement of the polishing drum causes the small roughly-cut tubings of beads to rub against one another, as well as against the little grains of sand added in to produce extra abrasive effect. The process is not unlike the grinding action of sands on the seashore produced by the rolling and tumbling motions of waves, except that in this case, the grinding action is confined inside a drum.

When the beads finally emerge from these drums, they are in the shape of oblates, i.e. little spheroids. It is, of course, possible to make beads of spherical or ellipsoidal shapes, but these are usually done with glass beads of much larger sizes, say, from 5 mm to 15 mm, and which are intended for making necklaces, bracelets and other articles of personal ornament requiring large and showy beads.

The kinds of threads used

Unlike modern beadwork which employs nylon threads of different sizes more extensively nowadays for stringing, threading, weaving and stitching beads, traditional Straits Chinese beaded ornaments were, without exception, fabricated entirely with the aid of cotton threads. Nylon threads were, of course, unknown during the nineteenth century and the first half of the twentieth century. But silk threads, though avail-

able, were never used, mainly because they were relatively more expensive.

Now the use of twisted or drawn cotton threads of different thickness and strengths for stringing, and especially threading, of beadwork, with the help of fine needles, actually requires more skill than is apparent to the uninitiated. This is because cotton threads – unless previously treated with beeswax or candlewax, have an irritating tendency to tangle and foul up the works. This can happen when the needle is required to pass through the bead a second or third time in opposite directions.

Silk threads are smoother and have greater tensile strength than cotton threads. But whether for reasons of economy, ingrained conservatism or convenience, the traditional nonyas always used very fine strands of cotton threads for stitching, threading and stringing. Indeed, the tassels of most old beadwork are the weakest parts of these ornaments, and they snap off easily when old cotton threads get frayed. Had the nonyas used thicker and multi-stranded cotton threads (but then the stringing process would have slowed down considerably) more pieces of old Straits Chinese beadwork would have survived to this day.

Cotton threads not only lose their tensile strength with passing time, but are subject to attack by fungi, mites, silverfish and cockroaches, not to mention the effects of humidity in the tropics. The result is that most extant pieces dating mostly between the late nineteenth and the first two decades of the twentieth century, have all begun to show various signs of decay, such as patches of missing beads, broken cotton threads, frayed edges, discoloured velvet and cotton or flannel backings.

No beadwork from Penang, Malacca and Singapore are likely to be older than a century. No authenticated eighteenth-century pieces are known to have survived in Malacca (Penang was founded in 1796 and Singapore in 1819) even though the nonyas must have learnt the techniques of stringing, threading and stitching beads from the Malays long before the coming of the British and the great influx of Chinese immigrants to the Straits Settlements at the beginning of the nineteenth century.

Most extant pieces of Straits Chinese beadwork are between 60 and 90 years at the most, and many have already begun to show signs of deterioration due to frayed and broken cotton threads. Had silk threads been used, most of the beadwork would probably have been better preserved, other things being equal.

Weight for weight, silk threads have greater tensile strength and last infinitely longer than cotton threads. In fact, if silk threads or silk fabrics are properly preserved, they can last up to two thousand years or more. This is shown by the fact that a painted T-shaped silk banner recovered from the intact tomb of a certain Madam Li Tsang, wife of the Marquis of Tai in Changsha, Hunan, in 1972, was dated to the time of the Western Han dynasty (206 B.C.–A.D. 24). Fifty other pieces of silk fabrics in fine condition were also found with this silk banner.[11]

Since Rocaille beads used in Straits Chinese beadwork were extremely small (between 0.5 mm and 1 mm in diameter), the stitching and threading of these beads require not only excellent eyesight but also prolonged concentration, especially in fabricating articles with intricate designs. Progress is usually slow even for a skilled worker because, amongst other things, a considerable number of beads are required to cover one square inch of space.

Assuming that the average diameter of a Rocaille bead, size 8 or 7, is 1 mm in size, then in order to fill one square inch, one actually needs to stitch or thread together a total of 625 beads. It follows that in order to fabricate a decorative beaded panel measuring no more than 5.6 inches by 9.6 inches or, in other words, 53.76 square inches, one would need a total of something like 33,600 beads!

The largest extant beaded panel in Straits Chinese beadwork is that broad bed-runner attached to the mattress of the wedding bed, and it measures, on the average, 72 inches by 6 inches, or in other words, 432 square inches. Since each square inch of beaded work requires approximately 625 Rocaille beads, the entire mattress panel would require an incredible total of 270,000 beads!

If, for the sake of argument, we assume that on the average a skilled beadworker takes three seconds to stitch one bead into position (this estimated time allows for lapses of attention, delays caused by picking up the wrong beads, threading of needles, fouling of threads and pauses), then 270,000 beads would require a total of 810,000 seconds, or 225 hours of steady and regular work. Let us suppose that a beadworker devotes an average of 4 hours of consistent work per day to the task. In that case, she would take 56¼ days to finish the work of beading. If another 3 or 4 days are taken in the cutting and sewing (by hand) of the several layers of cotton-and-velvet backing, it will take 60 days altogether to complete a beaded mattress panel.

In reality, the job would probably have taken a longer time, probably 2½ months, especially if the beadworker works at a more leisurely pace, with frequent pauses for snatches of conversation, food and drinks, to rest tired eyes and so on. Workers, unlike machines, get bored, tired and inattentive, and beadwork, if one has watched the old nonyas at work, gets to be tedious and tiresome as the days go by.

Needles

The needles used for threading and stitching fine beadwork are very similar, if not identical, with those used for embroidery. These needles are extremely thin and relatively long (about 3 to 3.5

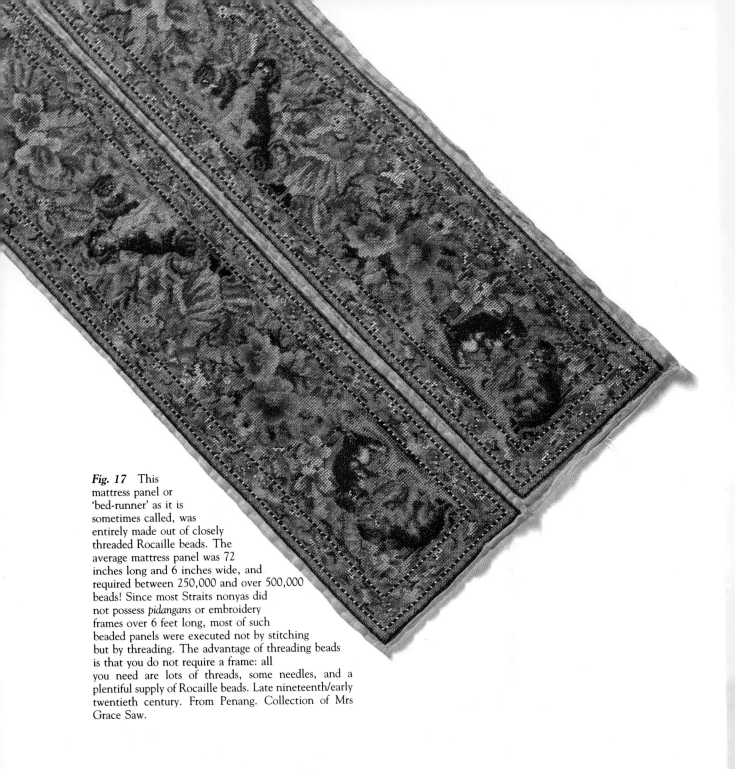

Fig. 17 This mattress panel or 'bed-runner' as it is sometimes called, was entirely made out of closely threaded Rocaille beads. The average mattress panel was 72 inches long and 6 inches wide, and required between 250,000 and over 500,000 beads! Since most Straits nonyas did not possess *pidangans* or embroidery frames over 6 feet long, most of such beaded panels were executed not by stitching but by threading. The advantage of threading beads is that you do not require a frame: all you need are lots of threads, some needles, and a plentiful supply of Rocaille beads. Late nineteenth/early twentieth century. From Penang. Collection of Mrs Grace Saw.

cm in length), and the eye is no bigger than the full-stop here.

Needles, like Rocaille beads, are graded in descending order, say, from 'No. 12' to 'No. 2' – the bigger the number, the finer the needle. Because these needles are made of iron, they have to be specially packed in silver foils in bundles of ten and then inserted into small, cylindrical metal containers. Others are inserted into rectangular pieces of double-folded silver foils, laid out in parallels, and then folded with a variety of thick black paper.

Two common brands of antique needles, namely, 'Kirby Nephus Ultra needles' of Kirby, Beard & Co., and 'Sharps No. 12 Milward' of Milward in Redditch, were of English origin. The majority of Straits Chinese beaded ornaments were stitched or threaded by the use of No. 12 or No. 13 Kirby or Sharps needles. Needless to say, these are highly brittle and break easily.

5
Techniques of Beading

THE ART OF beadwork and embroidery was a domestic skill which most traditional nonya girls learnt from their mothers and grandmothers, and probably their aunts and grand-aunts as well. They did not attend special schools to learn skills of embroidery, or of stringing or threading beads.

Before the turn of the century, girls stayed at home. If, for some reason, the wealthier Straits Chinese families considered it necessary to educate their daughters in English, private tutors (and female teachers only!) were engaged to teach them the three R's, namely, Reading, Writing and Arithmetic.

Traditionally, then, the art of beadwork and embroidery was a skill handed down from mother to daughter. Since the house-proud nonya was an exacting tutor (and some of my female cousins readily admitted that their mothers twisted their ears, pinched their backs blue and black, and pulled their hair, when they fumbled or blundered), years of slow and persistent tutoring must have gone to ensure that their daughters had mastered the finer points of the art.

Those who have grown up in a Straits Chinese family will know that just as the traditional nonya took great pride (and pains) in her culinary art, she demanded no less uncompromisingly that her daughters' embroidered and beaded ornaments should meet the highest possible degree of artistry and refinement. This insistence on excellence was,

to a large extent, reinforced by the habit of the nonyas to view one another's accomplishments in these homely arts and crafts with a very critical eye. Thus, in order not to 'lose face' in the eyes of their friends, relatives and neighbours, they had to ensure that only the best beadwork and embroidery were displayed in their homes during a wedding celebration.

Methods of Beading

Of the four standard methods of beading universally employed by skilled beadworkers all over the world since time immemorial, namely, stringing, threading (also known as 'stripwork' or 'chains'), stitching and weaving, only the first three techniques appeared to have been widely used in Straits Chinese beadwork.

As far as I have been able to ascertain, the nonyas seemed to have deliberately avoided applying the technique of weaving beads; and this is borne out by the fact that I have never, in the past fifteen years, encountered anything resembling a bead-loom in any old Straits Chinese home. Nor, for that matter, has a bead-loom ever surfaced in a local antique shop in Malaysia. Square, rectangular and circular stretchers and frames are occasionally encountered among the bric-à-brac kept in

SLIP KNOT

some disused store-rooms, but bead-looms were conspicuously absent.

Why this should be so is not clear to me. After all, the Ibans, the Kelabits, the Muruts, the Kayans, the Sea Dayaks, the Kadazans and other tribes of Sabah and Sarawak have successfully employed this technique of weaving beads to produce a fascinating variety of decorative and utilitarian articles. My own guess is that the Straits Chinese scrupulously avoided weaving because they considered it as menial work. This aversion to manual work seemed to have been an ingrained cultural trait of the Straits Chinese; indeed, no young baba would ever consider making a living out of carpentry, wood-carving, farming, fishing, brick-laying or even fire-fighting.

Stringing

The first thing that the student of beadwork learns, is how to string beads together to produce an aesthetic design in the form of a simple bracelet or a necklace. This, of course, implies that the novice must learn two basic steps, namely, how to thread a needle (and embroidery and beadwork needles are fine and have eyes which are considerably smaller than ordinary sewing needles), and how to tie a knot.

There are several ways to make a knot with thread and needle. The usual method employed by most Chinese housewives is to hold down one end of the thread by pressing the left thumb against the index finger, and making several turns of the thread around the tip of the finger. By means of the right index finger and thumb, she makes several turns of the thread around the left index finger. Next, using the left thumb, she rolls the several loops of thread until they reach the tips of the index finger and thumb. With the right index finger and thumb, the embroiderer now pulls the

other end of the thread away until the loops on the left hand have tightened into a knot.

The other way is to make several loose loops of the thread by running the needle in an up-and-down movement in different directions and then pulling tight by holding on to the loose end of the thread. The result is a slip knot. The slip knot is particularly useful for securing and joining threads together.

The novice has to practise these elementary but fundamental steps in stringing until she has acquired sufficient proficiency in the use of thread and needle to create a variety of designs. Careful study of tribal beadwork will show that an endless variety of designs can be created with this technique.

While the technique of stringing beads to create ornamental objects was thoroughly familiar to the nonyas, most extant samples of Straits Chinese beadwork were not fabricated exclusively by the bead-stringing method. This is not entirely surprising, seeing that the beaded articles most amenable to the technique of bead-stringing, including such items as chokers of various designs, necklaces made out of a variety of beads of different sizes, shapes and materials, bracelets, anklets, earrings, etc., never became fashionable with the nonyas.

They were indeed very fond of beaded ornaments for display and decoration on ceremonial occasions, but they did not fancy themselves being decked with elaborate items of personal jewellery made out of ordinary glass beads after the fashion of the Dayaks, the Ibans, the Kayans or the Orang Asli (or Aborigines). As urbanites belonging to the community of merchants and traders, they preferred the more expensive types of jewellery crafted out of gold and precious stones. Besides, such items of jewellery had higher marketable value.

Stitching

The most prevalent type of Straits Chinese bead-work in extant happen to be executed by the technique of stitching. Strictly speaking, however, stitching is regarded as intrinsic to the art of embroidery rather than that of beadwork, in the sense that the basic skill required for executing stitched beads is no different from that required for sewing a simple stitch in needlework.

But no matter: many of the most fascinating pieces of Straits Chinese beadwork were created by simply stitching one by one, with the help of Sharps embroidery needles and single-stranded cotton threads, tens of thousands of tiny Rocaille beads on to patterns copied on velvet, cotton, canvas or flannel materials which have been tightly stretched out on a square, rectangular, or even a circular 'tambour' frame (see fig. 18). The technique was essentially the same as that of making *petit point* stitches with needle and thread, except that instead of using fine, smooth and shiny silk threads, the beadworker sewed little beads of different colours and textures on the surface design to create various pleasing patterns.

Embroidery frames

In stitching or embroidering beads, the beadworker must first trace the entire outline of the design in white (if the fabric happens to be of a dark colour) on to the fabric – velvet was often preferred to other materials. The fabric intended for embroidery must be strengthened and stiffened by pasting several layers of thin cotton and gauze-like materials on to its underside. The treated fabric must be thoroughly dried and then ironed till it is smooth and flat.

Next, the fabric is mounted on to one of those wooden, rectangular embroidery frames known as *pidangan*, *pedangan*, or *pinidangan*, as it is known in Bahasa. Since the embroidery frame is an essential part of the working apparatus of the art of

Fig. 18 A beaded-cum-embroidered panel. This unusual work, again the handicraft of some bygone generation of Penang nonyas, measures about 3 feet long and 10 inches wide, was fabricated in three separate panels and then joined together. What makes it unique, however, is that the apricot red background of this panel is made up entirely of cross stitches, while the figures and floral/foliated motifs were stitched with Rocaille beads. The stiffness in the motifs gives this panel an archaic appearance. But it is probably of late nineteenth or early twentieth century dating. From Penang. Collection of Mrs Ho Wing Meng.

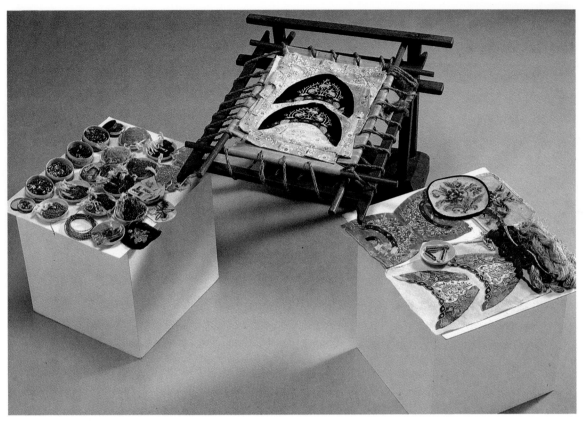

Fig. 19 A traditional Straits Chinese *pidangan* or embroidery frame, showing a pair of crescent-shaped embroidered coverings for a pair of nonya slippers mounted in readiness for stitchery work. On the left of the *pidangan*, can be seen small porcelain trays containing Rocaille beads, sequins, gold wires, and metal beads. On the right side of the *pidangan* are samples of partially embroidered crescent panels meant for wedding slippers, some patterns and a pile of silk threads. Properties of various people including Mr Peter Wee and Mrs Ho Wing Meng.

needlework, I should like to describe briefly how it is constructed and how it operates (see fig. 19).

Strictly speaking, the *pidangan* refers only to the embroidery frame used by the traditional nonyas to execute their various embroidered artefacts. Actually, the *pidangan* used by the nonyas consists of two sets of embroidery frames.

The first consists of a fixed and rigid rectangular wooden frame made of teakwood in which the four ends of the lengthwise bars jut several inches beyond the two connecting transverse or widthwise bars. These protruding ends allow the frame to be slotted into the space provided by the upright supports of the accompanying needle-box.

The second frame which is movable and adjustable consists of four thin, tubular wooden sticks whose lengths and widths correspond with those of the fixed frame. These four movable sticks are usually inserted into the narrow border sleeves of a rectangular piece of strong cotton fabric into which a rectangular hole has been cut out at the centre, and placed over the top of the fixed frame. Next the movable frame is tacked on to the fixed frame by means of strings which are executed in zig-zag fashion.

The traditional Straits Chinese embroidery frame is always accompanied by a wooden rectangular needle-box consisting of a rectangular casing of about 16 inches long, 7 inches wide and 8 inches high, with three built-in drawers arranged in two tiers, the two smaller drawers being placed above the single, larger drawer below. These drawers were used to keep beads, needles, threads, thimble, scissors and other odds and ends.

Four upright posts rising out of the corners of this rectangular case are secured lengthwise at the top by two horizontal bars arranged parallel to each other. The 'front' wooden bar is 16 inches high, while the one at the back is 18 inches high, and the ends which jut a few inches out of their vertical

Fig. 20 A pair of crescent-shaped beaded coverings for nonya slippers. Notice that on these two panels the stitching of the beads to the figure motifs and the background has been completed. The designs on these panels are, however, more modern than traditional in taste. Collection of Mr Peter Wee.

rectangular frame used by embroiderers in Britain and elsewhere in this respect. While the slate frame is a large picture-like frame attached to the inner sides of the two upright posts of a U-shaped wooden support by swivelling hinges which enable the frame to be tilted at any angle, the *pidangan* was rigidly fixed in a horizontal position.

Now in addition to the outlines of the entire design traced upon the fabric (usually dark-coloured velvets such as maroon reds, green, blue and violet), the embroiderer utilized a duplicate of the pattern in which the positioning of the beads was indicated by silk stitches or stitched beads of different colours (see figs. 19 & 20).

The duplicate patterns indicating the positioning of the beads were always done on a type of fine cotton gauze in which the double-stranded warps and woofs are crossed at 1-mm intervals to form a fine network. The beads are *never* stitched horizontally or vertically along the warp or the woof, but always *obliquely* at the point where the warp and woof *cross* each other. This, I suppose, was done for a practical purpose, as the point at which the warp and woof threads cross is also the strongest part of the fabric for anchoring the beads down. However, by a happy coincidence, this askew positioning of the beads, apparently dictated by a practical consideration, has given old Straits Chinese stitched beadwork a more pleasing and elegant appearance.

Had the technique of stitching been confined to an up-and-down or left-and-right positioning of the beads, the patterns would have emerged looking so much stiffer and more rigid. Even when the Rocaille beads were stitched on to a velvet fabric without the benefit of a fine network of warps and woofs to guide one in the positioning of the beads, the nonyas adhered to the principle of arranging their beads in an askew fashion.

This oblique positioning of the beads, undoubtedly pleasing in itself, is further highlighted

supports at either end, are sometimes carved with dragon heads and gilded with gold foils. Now the difference between the height of the frontal bar and that of the back bar was deliberately made to provide a slotting space for the jutting ends of the fixed rectangular *pidangan* to be inserted into the space between the two horizontal bars. When fitted into position, the *pidangan* lies in a flat, horizontal plane – which is how the frame looks when it is in working position.

In the old days, the nonyas always sat on the floor when working with a piece of embroidery. Hence, the heights of the upright supports of the needle-box have to be between 18 inches and 16 inches to provide a comfortable working level.

Since the *pidangan* and its accompanying needle-box was traditionally presented to the bride, and every desirable bride in those days was expected to excel in the art of embroidery and beadwork, the needle-box was always painted in auspicious red lacquer with gold outlines. It is clear, therefore, that the traditional *pidangan* used by the Straits nonyas differs from the slate or by an accident of the manufacturing process, in which the uneven action of abrasives inside the rotatory, polishing drums, caused facetings to appear on the surface of what would otherwise have been smooth, spheroidal beads.

Facetings of this sort, it was soon realized, made Rocaille beads shimmer and glitter attractively, especially when they are closely stitched or threaded *en masse*. This fact did not escape the aesthetic sensibility of traditional Straits nonyas who exploited the brilliant effect of faceted Rocaille beads to maximum effect on all their ceremonial beaded artefacts. And such was their esteem for this type of beads that they named it *manek potong* (literally, cut beads) to distinguish it from other types of Rocaille beads, to which they gave the common name, *manek kacha*, i.e. 'glass beads', with a derogatory hint attached to it. What the nonyas (and the babas as well) probably did not realize was that, what they designated as *manek potong*, was not a special grade of Rocaille beads intended by the bead manufacturers in Lyons as such, but rather a manufacturing defect which caused between 10 and 15 per cent of Rocaille beads to be faceted.

The fabric intended for the beads to be stitched upon is never used singly for stretching out upon the *pidangan*, until it has been suitably stiffened and strengthened by three or four layers of gauze-like cotton fabrics pasted to its underside. Because glass beads are heavy, when several tens of thousands are used to decorate a piece of fabric, they can exert an intolerable amount of pressure, causing the warps and woofs to come apart. Adequate stiffening of the fabric is thus necessary to hold the beads securely in place.

In any case, when employing the technique of stitched beads, the Straits nonya displayed the same uncompromising care as regards attention to detail, richness of colours, beauty of designs and neatness of workmanship. Usually the beads are stitched so closely together that the texture is almost similar to that seen in woven beads; except that in this case, the designs are not arranged in parallels, but depicted in intricate patterns.

With as many as 625 beads crammed into one square inch of space, when the beads are actually stitched that compactly on to a velvet backing, they create a complex network of thousands of stitches criss-crossing one another in every direction on the under-surface of the fabric.

That is why a typical sample of Straits Chinese beadwork executed by stitching, is a very strong and durable piece of craftsmanship, besides having a scintillating old-world charm of its own. Thus, if well-preserved by being kept away from excessive moisture, and protected from fungi and insects, it can last a long time, even though each individual bead is secured by nothing more than a single, fragile strand of cotton thread. Indeed, some of the extant wedding slippers with pointed toe-covers made entirely out of stitched beads, and reputed to be more than 80 years old, are still in a fine state of preservation, except for a certain amount of tarnishing of the silver threads, if these happened to be used, and the fading of the coloured silk threads.

Threading

Of the three most common methods of working with beads, namely, stringing, stitching and threading, threading (also known as 'stripwork' or simply 'chains'), appeared to have been extremely popular, especially with the former generations of Penang nonyas. Threaded beadwork is, of course, found in Malacca and Singapore, but whereas the old Malacca and Singapore nonyas were content to use the art of threading beads merely to make decorative fringes or borders with short simple tassels for their silk embroidered panels, the Penang nonyas created an incredible variety of

Fig. 21 Rectangular panel executed entirely by threading, except for the tassels. The background of this panel is unusual for the pearly white tone which it conveys, while the decorative designs formalized in geometric patterns remind one of woven fabrics done by aborigine tribes in Indonesia. This panel, however, was the handiwork of a Penang nonya – which goes to show that despite their lack of formal schooling and professional training, the nonyas, left to their own devices, were able to create artefacts of imaginative and innovative beauty. Dimensions: 14 inches (including tassels) × 10 inches. From Penang. Collection of Mrs Grace Saw.

decorative objects and panels rarely seen in Malacca and Singapore.

Indeed, if we are to judge by the frequency with which beadwork occurs in old Straits Chinese homes in Penang (and the bulk of the best surviving pieces come from this island), we must conclude that the Straits Chinese of Penang, more than their counterparts in Malacca and Singapore, made a fine art out of beadwork. Most people who were introduced to old nonya beadwork from Penang for the first time (and Mrs Grace Saw, whose family formerly ran an embroidery-cum-beadwork shop in Georgetown, possesses one of the finest collections of Penang beadwork) were quite astonished at the brilliant intricacy and breathtaking beauty of these works. Those who have examined these gorgeous beadwork in detail, were left in no doubt that the former generations of

Penang ladies greatly excelled in the art of threading beads (see fig. 21).

The main thing about the technique of threading beads is that it requires no cumbersome equipment in the form of stretchers and frames of different shapes and sizes, or for that matter, any preparatory work associated with the stiffening, strengthening and straightening of the fabric, sketching or tracing out of the design and mounting the fabric on the frames. All that one needs, other than an assorted selection of Rocaille beads, is a needle and some cotton threads, plus a good eye for design and very dexterous fingers.

The design is not created *ad lib* as one goes along, but is copied from a prepared pattern indicating the position of the different beads and the colours to be employed. The pattern is always placed in front of the beadworker.

Techniques of Beading   55

If an amateur beadworker were to make a small beaded panel by applying the technique of threading beads, she will begin by threading out some geometric or conventionalized floral pattern intended for the border of the beaded panel. She can choose from one of the patterns shown in the above diagram. Using Rocaille beads of different colours, she will repeat the same threading procedure until she has produced a continuous chain, or strip, of the required length. When the first strip of border pattern has been threaded out, the beadworker goes back to the starting point immediately below, and threads out the same pattern which is now oriented in a downward direction.

This pattern is repeated only once (or at the most twice) to produce a border of similar width. Then a new pattern is begun, as indicated in the pattern-card, and the beadworker works her way from left to right until she judges there is just enough space left to end the strip by executing the original border pattern, also oriented in a downward direction.

In this way, the beadworker begins and ends each successive strip of beads with the original border pattern. The choice of designs in subsequent strips is, of course, determined by what is specified in the pattern-card. But as long as the designs are set out in regular geometric forms, or rather forms which are amenable to the regular positioning of the beads, the process of threading is orderly and does not call for complicated manoeuvres of needle and thread.

However, if the patterns turn out to be non-schematic, but irregular and somewhat naturalistic, as is the case with the complex designs of many extant pieces of Straits Chinese beadwork, the threading procedures become more complicated. And the more complex and irregular the patterns become, the more complex are the passes which must be executed as the needle and threads are made to pass through the same beads several times in opposite directions. This is where the problem of fouling and tangling of threads comes in. In the hands of a skilled beadworker, who is adept at controlling the working threads, tanglings are reduced to a minimum.

Fig. 22 A rectangular beaded panel entirely fabricated by the technique of threading. Typically Straits Chinese in taste, the designs are ornate (and threading out those arabesque floral and foliated motifs calls for skill, a sure hand and an eye for aesthetic design) and of strong colours – in this case red and blue floral motifs set against a background of pearly white beads. Collection of Mrs Grace Saw.

Another problem associated with threading is that when the needle and thread have gone through the correct passes without fouling, the thread must be pulled to tighten the beads into position. It is important at this juncture that the pressure with which the thread is pulled together should be equal and regular from the beginning to the end of the strip or chain of beaded patterns. If not, a beaded panel will exhibit the characteristic 'wrinkles' and corrugated foldings similar to the gathering effects of smocking on a gown or skirt.

Generally speaking, when a beaded panel contains beads of different sizes as well as intricate and irregular patterns, as is the case with many pieces of Straits Chinese beadwork, a certain amount of distortion is to be expected. But where the patterns are schematic and regular and the beads of uniform sizes, then a neat and well-threaded panel should show little or no distortion or wrinkling effects.

The challenge presented by the threading technique is that in the hands of a skilled worker using only needle, thread and a generous supply of Rocaille beads, an endless variety of fascinating designs can be created (see fig. 22). Anthropologists who have lived and worked among the various native tribes in Africa, Polynesia and Micronesia, have often praised the colour sense and inventive ingenuity of tribal, threaded beadwork.

It is my opinion that the reader who takes the trouble to study Straits Chinese beadwork, especially the pieces executed by threading, will be no less impressed by the exquisite craftsmanship, rich colours and exotic complexities of their designs. For whereas all tribal beadwork, irrespective of origin, whether it is in North America or Polynesia, have characteristically stiff, formalized and geometric patterns, Straits Chinese beadwork displays an incredible variety of naturalistic patterns and motifs.

And yet, for all their exquisite craftsmanship and beauty of design, not a single piece of Straits Chinese beadwork in extant bears the name or signature of its maker. Although the commercial-minded Chinese were not unmindful of the importance of reputable shop-names, brand-names and names of master craftsmen, not a single piece of extant nonya beadwork has a name attached to it.

Still, the anonymity of these artefacts does not make the slightest difference to the quality of their workmanship. Indeed, since these artefacts were made at home by the nonyas for their family members, they were created with no commercial or profit motives in mind. Being labours of love, superior craftsmanship was the sole criterion of excellence.

6
Categories of Straits Chinese Beadwork

IN DESCRIBING STRAITS Chinese beadwork, I propose to divide all extant examples into two broad categories: (1) personal ornaments of the bride, groom, the bridesmaid and the groom's attendant; and (2) decorative ornaments (by far the larger of the two categories) used to decorate the bridal chamber. However, the range of artefacts which may be included in each of these two broad categories is so varied as regards their shapes and specific functions that they may, to all intents and purposes, be regarded as different articles in their own right.

For example, under the category of 'Personal ornaments' may be included the following items: purses for the bride and groom; belts for the bride and groom; *selendang*, the ceremonial shoulder strip worn by the bride (and female relatives as well); *sapu tangan*, a triangular panel embroidered with beads and sequins on both sides, for the bride; elaborate head-pieces meant for the bridesmaid usually; broad circular collars with elaborate beaded designs also meant for the bridesmaid; knee-cap ornaments for the groom; narrow collar-like panels sewn to the brim of caps worn by the groom and the groom's attendant; and of course, beaded shoes and slippers for the bridal couple and their attendants. The only thing that these differently fabricated, beaded artefacts have in common, is that they were meant to be objects of personal adornment.

The same may be said of the various beaded artefacts that I have classified under 'Decorative ornaments' for the bridal chamber. Except for such things as containers for combs, hairpins and toiletries (made to be attached to the wall or the upright supports of the wash-stand), spectacle cases, candle-covers and gewgaws for attaching to the wedding bed, most of these decorative ornaments are in the forms of variously-shaped panels.

These panels were mostly executed by threading and stitching, and they included *bantal* plates or pillow ends (see fig. 24); table-covers; table-mats; elaborate hangings for the bridal wash-stand (see figs. 2, 8 & 11) with borders and elaborate tassels; embroidered panels hung from the lintels of doors and windows and the frontal carved panels of the four-poster wedding bed; pillow-covers; bed-runners or mattress panels; ogival panels for the tops of the pair of bridal footstools; circular panels for the tops of food-covers; narrow panels, long or short, for the extremities of the *selendang*; and ceremonial cloths for wrapping the bride's jewels, etc. Such ornamental beaded panels are among the most impressive examples of Straits Chinese beadwork.

Fig. 23 Handbag fabricated entirely out of colourful Rocaille beads stitched on to a backing of several layers of gauze and cotton. This bag came from Penang and differs somewhat from handbags of similar designs in peranakan Chinese homes in Indonesia: the colours are brighter. Collection of Mrs Grace Saw.

Fig. 24 The four specimens of three types of embroidered *bantal* plates shown here are more typically Straits Chinese in taste though they originated in Indonesia and were reputedly made by the peranakan Chinese there. There is evidence to show that embroidered *bantal* plates, whether of silk, gold threads or Rocaille beads, were more commonly used by Indonesian peranakan Chinese than, say, silver *bantal* plates. My personal experience led me to conclude that the Straits Chinese in Peninsular Malaya preferred silver *bantal* plates to embroidered ones. Collection of Donald Harper.

Fig. 25 A bead embroidered belt of maroon background and two examples of embroidered wedding purses. The purses shown here are similar to those made by peranakan Chinese in Indonesia. Late nineteenth/early twentieth century. From Singapore. Collection of Mr Peter Wee.

Fig. 26 Beaded handbag executed by threading. From about the end of the nineteenth century to the early decades of the present century (up to the late twenties), handbags of such European designs became popular with the Straits nonyas, although they still adhered to the traditional handbags or wallets during their wedding ceremonies. This handbag is probably of Victorian or Edwardian period. Collection of Mrs Grace Saw.

PERSONAL ORNAMENTS

Although the tradition of using Rocaille beads to fabricate both personal and decorative beaded ornaments in the Straits Chinese community was largely derived from the customs of the Minangkabau Malays, the uses which most of these articles were put to, were recognizably Chinese in origin.

However, the extensive use of beads for making ceremonial artefacts intended for weddings, was never adopted in China – the traditional Chinese preferred to embroider their most cherished objects in silk threads rather than have them fabricated out of glass beads. In this respect, the Straits Chinese were unique in their wedding customs.

For example, those pouch-shaped purses (see fig. 25) embroidered with beads and sequins or appliquéd with ornate gilded silver panels (see figs. 72 & 73 on pages 100-101 in *Straits Chinese Silver*) are similar to silk-embroidered purses made in China, except that the Straits Chinese modified the more conventional square or rectangular shapes to pouch-like shapes. Similarly, the beaded belts (see also fig. 25) stitched on velvet panels and stiffened with several layers of cotton fabrics pasted on the reverse side, were similar to silk-embroidered belts made in China; and so, too, are those narrow collar-like beaded panels sewn around the brims of caps worn by the groom and groom's attendant, except that the traditional Chinese did not use

Rocaille beads.

Purses of this type are, of course, traditionally Chinese in taste, and they were all made in such a way that they could be slotted into the beaded belt worn by both the bride and groom when clothed in their formal and elaborately embroidered costumes. But from about the nineteenth century to the 1930s, the nonyas began to use handbags fabricated entirely out of threaded and/or stitched glass beads, and fashioned after the manner of Victorian or Edwardian handbags. Some of these handbags (see fig. 26) were imported from Britain.

While most of these artefacts had their counterparts in China, others were peculiar to Straits Chinese wedding customs. These are the *sapu tangan* ornament (see fig. 65), broad-rim collars, head-pieces, *selendang*, and the ubiquitous beaded slippers and shoes. The traditional Chinese bridal couple and attendants did not have such articles among their repertoire of personal ornaments.

The *sapu tangan* and *selendang* are uniquely Malay in origin, and so is the impressive head-piece (seen in Minangkabau wedding rituals) worn by the bridesmaid (see fig. 27) as well as the *tempat sireh* (see fig. 28). The magnificent beaded collar, worn only by the bridesmaid, bears some resemblance to those broad and multi-layered collars worn by African native women.

Fig. 27 *Selendang* and head-pieces for a traditional Straits Chinese wedding. The magnificent damask cloths, almost two feet square, are not handkerchiefs but *selendang*, or ornamental shoulder cloths. But these pieces were meant for older nonyas clad in *baju panjang* (a variation of the *sarung kebaya* in which the 'kebaya' reaches down below the knee). The older nonyas usually fold these square cloths into a triangle, attaching one end to the topmost *kerosang* or brooch, and draping the other end over the shoulder. The two beaded head-pieces shown here were traditionally worn by the two bridal attendants, a boy and a girl. Collection of Mr Peter Wee.

Fig. 28 This cone-shaped, iron container fitted with a matching jacket of Rocaille beads stitched to a black velvet backing, was a traditional receptacle for *sireh* leaves, and known in Baba Malay as *tempat sireh*. This one is of Indonesian origin, and the beaded jacket was made by nonyas in Java. Length: 7 inches. Collection of Donald Harper.

Fig. 29 Six pairs of old *kasut manek* done in two different styles: one type having low heels, i.e. *kasut tumit*, and the other which is flat, is known as *kasut seret*. The embroidered bead-patterns on the toe-covers of all six pairs of *kasut manek* are apparently of vintage workmanship, but their soles (with the exception of the soles of the pair of slippers with blue bead background) have all been refurbished. Courtesy of Mr Peter Wee.

Kasut manek

Concerning the pair of beaded slippers which every traditional nonya wore in conjunction with her *sarung kebaya* or *baju panjang*, this was an essential item of their national dress (see fig. 29). These slippers are known as *kasut manek*, meaning literally, 'beaded shoes'. Some of the older nonyas who are still alive today may own several pairs of these beaded slippers, some of which may be over fifty or sixty years old.

Kasut manek dating back to the early twentieth century are probably still around, though there is no way of determining their age based on stylistic evidence alone. Such vintage beaded slippers were greatly treasured by most nonyas of a bygone generation. They took great care to wrap their *kasut manek* in cotton cloths stuffed with some dried pepper seeds or mothballs and then stored them away in pig-skin or camphor-wood chests. Vintage *kasut manek* were worn only on important ceremonial occasions.

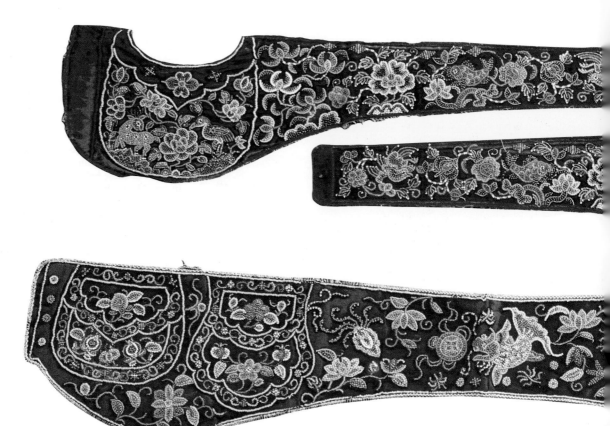

shorter, separate parts – each of which was mounted on a standard *pidangan*, and then stitched together to form the belt.

An examination of most existing specimens of antique beaded belts clearly shows that all the belts were actually made of two separate panels joined together by stitching. As with other categories of beadwork, Rocaille beads were used. Occasionally, however, one comes across velvet belts stitched with rare, faceted metal beads (again of French make) hardly more than 0.5 mm in size. Belts ornamented with metal beads are rare but very impressive to look at.

Head-piece

The beaded head-piece (see fig. 32) made for the traditional bridesmaid, is among the more curious examples of Straits Chinese beadwork. But unlike belts, slippers, collars, *selendang*, *sapu tangan* and caps, there was no standard shape for this ceremonial head-dress other than the circular head-band which is made to fit into the crown of the head.

Once the basic head-band panel has been constructed, appliquéd ornamental patterns of various sorts including *ju-i* heads, butterflies, auspicious fruits (e.g. pomegranates, peaches, finger citrons) and flower baskets could be attached to the circular head-band. These appliquéd ornaments are fabricated separately and then tacked on to the inner side of the head-band. The most prominent appliquéd ornaments would be stitched directly over the forehead.

Head-pieces of this type look like coronets minus the glint of gold. As with other ornaments, the beaded patterns were invariably stitched with small Rocaille beads; in some pieces both the obverse and reverse sides were covered with beads.

Fig. 31 Two examples of bead-embroidered wedding belts with built-in purses. Notice that these belts are not cut in the shape of a thin rectangular strip, but bulges outwards where the built-in purses are positioned. This was probably an Indonesian innovation of the traditional Straits Chinese wedding belts which were invariably fabricated independent of the purses. It is likely though that these belts were worn by the bridal attendants rather than either the bride or groom. They were shorter, being about 18 inches in length. Collection of Donald Harper.

Fig. 32 Ceremonial head-dress crafted in the shape of a *ju-i* symbol is ornamented with studs and sequins of gold and tassels of Rocaille beads set against a green velvet backing. Head-dresses of this sort were usually worn by bridal attendants. Length: 12 inches. From Indonesia. Collection of Donald Harper.

Fig. 33 Circular segment of embroidered bead collar executed entirely by stitching of tiny metal beads no bigger than 0.5 mm. Collars of this type were usually attached to the ceremonial embroidered costume of the flower girl who traditionally accompanied the bride. This collar came from an old family heirloom in Malacca. Late nineteenth century. Collection of Mrs Ho Wing Meng.

Collars

Collars are of two types: those which consisted of two semi-circular bands of stiffened velvets, between 1 and 1¼ inches wide, ornamented with beaded designs and traditionally stitched on to the plain satin collars of the tunic worn by the groom's attendant; and a broad circular band of between 4 and 5 inches width, made of stiffened velvet, and traditionally used by the bridesmaid (see fig. 33). The broad-rimmed collar made for the bridesmaid was by far the more impressive. Collars designed on the pattern of the circular band, or series of concentric bands, and entirely threaded or stitched with beads, are among the most ancient collar designs going back to the Egyptian Pharaonic era. The Straits Chinese version of these broad, circular collar bands are different from those used by African natives, as well as those made for the pharaohs and their queens.

Tribal collars are made up of several broad, concentric bands mounted over one another, and they are threaded with metal wires to stiffen them into the characteristic disc-shape. Pharaonic collars, on the other hand, are made in one broad, flat disc with several concentric rows of large tubular faience beads threaded into position. The large faience beads employed here are of different colours and they are arranged in geometric patterns of great simplicity.

Collar bands of this sort in ancient Egypt were insignias of royal and divine powers. By contrast, Straits Chinese collar bands are purely ornamental in function. They consist of a circular disc made out of stiffened velvet backing. The surface is decorated with bird and floral motifs stitched with small Rocaille and metal beads. Their function is purely ornamental.

Fig. 34 A rectangular panel of densely threaded beads in sombre colours. As with silk embroidered panels of this sort, this beaded panel was apparently used to cover the top of a blackwood tea-table. Length: 13 inches. Width: 10 inches. Late nineteenth/early twentieth century. From Penang. Collection of Mrs Grace Saw.

DECORATIVE ORNAMENTS

Ornamental panels

Of all extant examples of decorative beaded ornaments, the most characteristic pieces are rectangular panels of different sizes. In most cases, these panels were fabricated by the method of threading beads, although it was not unusual that in some pieces the designs were created entirely out of stitched beads. Square, circular, triangular and quatrefoil shapes are sometimes seen among old beadwork, but they are much less common than the rectangular ones.

Some of the largest and most intricate pieces of Straits Chinese beadwork were created with nothing more complex than a needle, lots of cotton threads, and several pounds of fine Rocaille beads. As I have already described previously (see page 47), to thread one of those bed-runners intended for the wedding bed measuring 72 inches by 6 inches, using Rocaille beads measuring 1 mm in diameter, required at least 270,000 beads. However, if faceted metal beads of only 0.5 mm thick had been used to thread the same bed-runner, the number of beads required would have amounted to 540,000, while the estimated time required to fabricate this panel would also have doubled, namely, 120 days or four months of steady work!

Fortunately, perhaps, most of the extant pieces of threaded as well as stitched beadwork are of smaller dimensions, as for example, table-mats (see fig. 34), small table-covers for blackwood tea-tables, ornamental hangings and narrow fringes, with or without tassels, tacked to larger, silk-embroidered panels to serve as ornamental finishings. Nevertheless, no matter what the sizes of these beaded panels might be, they all appeared to have been crafted with painstaking attention to detail.

As with all things made to nonya specifications, or else made by the nonyas themselves, the costs of the basic materials (in this case, cotton threads, needles, a good supply of beads, some gold and silver threads, sequins, cotton gauzes and remnants of velvets) were negligible. But the prodigious labour, the time and most of all, the skill, that went into the crafting of these artefacts, cannot be measured in monetary terms, because it was purely a labour of love – the nonyas did not care to sell their handiwork for cash. This being the case, it is only appropriate that our appraisal of any piece of Straits Chinese beadwork (and embroidery as well) should not be measured in purely monetary terms, whether they concern the costs or the market value of the artefact in question, but more importantly, in terms of its craftsmanship. Is it, in other words, a thing of beauty?

Mattress panels or bed-runners

Concerning those long mattress panels or bed-runners (see fig. 17) which are fabricated either by stitching or threading of beads, it is not easy to say which of the two techniques requires more work and more skill. Some of the traditional nonyas were obviously more skilled at threading beads of very complex designs (and the patterns of such panels were invariably intricate) and hence, were more efficient at applying this technique of craftsmanship. Others were proficient in the art of stitching and thus, more likely to make a good job of it.

Nevertheless, each technique of beading calls for a different set of skills. Where threading of beads is concerned, the beadworker has to be adept at joining threads, tying endless knots, remembering the complicated sequences in which the individual beads must be positioned, and also at running the needle and thread back and forth without causing frequent tanglings and foulings of threads to stall the works.

On the other hand, if one were to examine the underside of the several layers of cotton-gauze backings of one of these mattress panels, the maze of countless cotton stitches criss-crossing in every direction (every stitch being executed by hand) will boggle the mind. This becomes even more apparent when one examines the complex patterns on the obverse side, and notes how very closely the individual beads are packed together to form a dense and continuous surface of shimmering beads, every one of which is positioned in correct sequence.

For efficiency-conscious people who complain that work of this sort is of very low productivity, one can only reply that such handicrafts cannot be mass-produced. Hence, it makes no sense at all to talk about productivity – the catchword in all modern theories of economics – where a work of art is concerned.

Cut-work ornaments

Most panelled ornaments found in Straits Chinese beadwork are executed to produce a flat and even surface. But some of the beaded articles, such as those circular ornaments done in pierced work (see fig. 35) had parts of their designs raised in bold reliefs to create a three-dimensional effect.

The method employed goes somewhat as follows: first, the designs are traced on to a piece of prepared cotton fabric. Care is taken to ensure that those parts of the designs which are to be 'pierced' or cut-through are more widely spaced, while other parts which are raised in reliefs are enlarged slightly to make allowance for cotton-wool fillings to be stuffed underneath to create little swellings here and there.

Next, several pieces of thin cotton fabric are pasted underneath to provide a firm backing. The prepared design can now be stretched out on the standard *pidangan* or embroidery frame, and the stitching of the beads then commences.

When the stitching is completed, the embroidered fabric is taken off the *pidangan* and partially pasted on to a prepared piece of thin paper backing, while cotton wool is stuffed into those areas requiring a relief effect. The fabric is then

Fig. 35 The designs on the three circular beaded ornaments shown here are executed by a combination of stitching and cut-work. Two of the designs represent clusters of fruits, while the third depicts a spotted antelope browsing on *lingzhi* fungus in a bamboo forest. Articles of this sort were purely ornamental in function. Diameter: 6½ inches. Probably late nineteenth/early twentieth century. From Penang.

Fig. 36 Ornamental hangings, or gewgaws, for the traditional Straits Chinese wedding bed. The ornamental medallions usually come in sets of three arranged vertically and sporting long and colourful tassels. The ones shown here all came from old Straits Chinese homes in Penang. The huge and heavily constructed blackwood bed inlaid with mother-of-pearl designs is, however, not of Straits Chinese taste. Straits Chinese wedding beds were invariably made of *nam* wood and sport red and gold carvings. Collection of Mrs Grace Saw.

firmly glued to the paper backing and left to dry.

As many as eight sheets of paper may be pasted underneath to create a certain thickness of about 3.5 mm to the beaded ornament. The paper backing is now left to dry for several days. When it has been thoroughly dried, a puncher with razor-sharp edges resembling the operational end of a screwdriver is used to cut out the void spaces between the various decorative motifs until a cut-through or pierced work effect is achieved.

Gewgaws

Those ornaments which I have described elsewhere[13] as 'gewgaws' need not detain us for long, because the beaded counterparts of these articles appeared to have been uncommon even in Penang. They are usually fabricated in silk embroidery, or perhaps, in silvergilt. I am referring to those ornaments (see fig. 36) which are vertically strung together with elaborate tassels and spangles in sets of three objects representing the 'Three Abundances', *fu, lu, shou* or happiness, good luck and long life, or else, 'The Three Good Wishes', namely, *chang ming fu gui*, or long life, riches and honour.

These ornaments were always hung in pairs (a traditional wedding being an especially auspicious occasion) in conjunction with two necktie-shaped hangings before the entrance into the four-poster wedding bed. I have described these as 'gewgaws', but it is obvious from the fact that the various ornamental articles were meant to convey good wishes and happy tidings, that the traditional Straits Chinese did not regard them as purely decorative in function. After all, every motif used in traditional Chinese arts and crafts was intended

Fig. 37 Two beaded ornaments, known to Straits nonyas in Penang as 'comb boxes'. Whether ceremonial combs were actually kept in these receptacles has not been confirmed. The green ornamental receptacle on the left is executed by threading and stitching, while the maroon bead ornament is largely stitched with metal beads. Late nineteenth/early twentieth century. From Penang. Collection of Mrs Ho Wing Meng.

to stand for something favourable and propitious.

The procedures for making such 'gewgaws' are the same as those used in making the various beaded receptacles described below. First of all, the number of panels required to fabricate the various articles in the round (two, if the object is depicted as having only an obverse and a reverse side) are drawn or traced on to pre-stiffened pieces of velvet or cotton. If silk-thread embroidery motifs are required then a silk backing is necessary.

These panels are, as usual, then stretched out on embroidery frames and stitched with fine Rocaille beads in colours which replicate those in the original patterns. If only two identical panels are required, they are tacked together along the edges with some trimmings in such a way as to leave an opening, wherein cotton wool can be stuffed to give the article a certain bulge and solidity. Having done this, the edges are then stitched together.

Receptacles

Another method of working with beaded artefacts consists of making ornamental containers or receptacles of various shapes and sizes in which the beaded designs are either stitched or threaded into position. For example, in order to make an ornamental receptacle of the sort shown in fig. 37, the five separate panels (with the exception of the broad beaded panel with tassels attached to the base) which make up the completed article, are pre-fabricated on stiffened velvet panels and then tacked together.

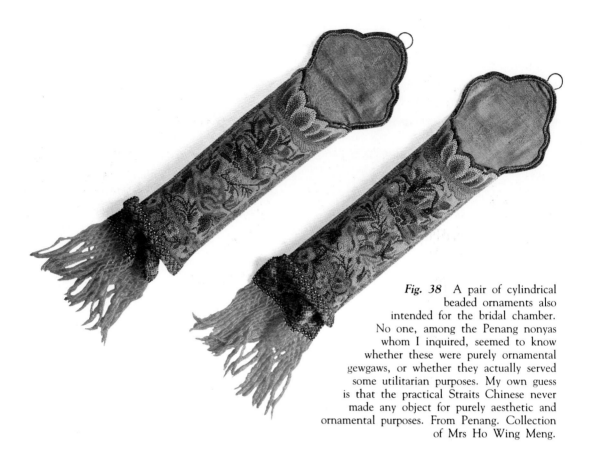

Fig. 38 A pair of cylindrical beaded ornaments also intended for the bridal chamber. No one, among the Penang nonyas whom I inquired, seemed to know whether these were purely ornamental gewgaws, or whether they actually served some utilitarian purposes. My own guess is that the practical Straits Chinese never made any object for purely aesthetic and ornamental purposes. From Penang. Collection of Mrs Ho Wing Meng.

This particular type of receptacle which is exclusively found in Penang is said to be a 'comb box', though it may be used to contain hairpins as well as ornamental combs used by the bride. Receptacles of this sort, including some which were purely cylindrical in shape (see fig. 38) appeared to have been fashionable only with the Penang nonyas, for they were rarely seen in Singapore or Malacca.

Penang beadwork

Indeed, I have noticed again and again over the years, that some of the most curious and impressive pieces of Straits Chinese beadwork invariably came from Penang. In the beginning, I relied mainly on information volunteered by collectors and dealers regarding the provenance of these types of beadwork. But by 1976, during a two-week holiday in Penang which was largely spent in discussions with several antique dealers, various establishments and

examining a large number of beadwork and embroidery brought to us by various people, it became easier to tell thereafter, whether a specimen of beadwork (and/or embroidery) was of Penang origin, merely by looking at the shape of the article in question, the style of the decorative design and the techniques of stitching and threading beads.

Penang workmanship had a distinctive characteristic about it: where the designs happen to consist of flowers, leaves and birds (mainly magpies and phoenixes), these motifs are usually depicted in a dense and crowded fashion with few empty spaces in between. The Penang style of rendering the tree-peony (*Paeonia lactiflora* and *Paeonia suffruticosa*) or 'Mou-tan' with their petals of rose-pink, lemon-yellow and crimson-red, reminds one of hybrid European roses rather than those splendid blossoms with loose and wavy petals of satin texture and colours of surpassing beauty, found in China (see fig. 39). These magnificent blossoms are often depicted in Canton embroider-

Fig. 39 Rectangular panel for blackwood tea-table executed entirely out of small Rocaille beads by threading. Notice that the handsome design depicting a spray of peonies set against a lovely blue background with zig-zag patterns, resembles roses rather than peonies. Fig. 1 shows a close-up view. Probably late nineteenth/early twentieth century. From Penang. Collection of Mrs Grace Saw.

ies with all the splendour befitting 'the King of Flowers'. The Penang peonies are however so different that when I saw them for the first time in 1970, I immediately mistook them for roses of the rose-pink variety with short and rounded petals. It was left to Mr Teo, a courteous and soft-spoken Teochew antique dealer, to correct me by saying that they were in fact meant to be peonies.

The distinctive Penang style of designs which is characterized by the preference for crowded and floral and foliated motifs with or without birds and phoenixes, is not exclusive to beadwork and embroidery. It is also to be seen in their red-and-gold or giltwood furniture made to Straits Chinese specifications. In fact, so distinctive is the Penang style of giltwood carvings seen in their furniture, that most students and collectors of the old, red-and-gold variety of Straits Chinese furniture (and there were in fact three types of such furniture) have no difficulty in identifying the Penang variety.

For some reason which I have not been able to explain satisfactorily, the traditional Straits Chinese families of Penang seemed to use far more beaded ornaments than their counterparts in Malacca and Singapore. It is true that such items like pillow-covers, ornamental hangings for the wedding bed (the so-called gewgaws), belts, ornamental head-gear for the bridesmaid, collars, *sapu tangan*, table-covers, bed-runners, beaded slippers, beaded purses, beaded knee-covers (for the groom), bridal stools, were found among the bridal trousseau of old Malacca and Singapore babas and nonyas.

But the Penang babas and nonyas tended to have a larger variety of beaded ornaments, including items not seen in old Malacca and Singapore homes. These are comb boxes, wall-panels, ornamental beaded-cum-embroidered panels for dressing mirrors and bridal wash-stands, *daun nipah* cigarette cases, beaded panels for tea-tables and pillows, pillow and bolster ends entirely fabricated in beadwork, and particularly, beaded borders and fringes for every conceivable type of embroidered panel. Indeed, students of Straits Chinese art will have noticed that for sheer ornateness of design, Penang workmanship surpasses that of either Singapore or Malacca Straits Chinese.

7
Peranakan Beadwork from Indonesia

THE BEADWORK WHICH I have referred to in the text thus far, have mostly been of Straits Chinese origin, and they came mainly from traditional Straits Chinese homes, or else from antique dealers who dealt largely with antiques and other bygones of Straits Chinese provenance. I also referred to old Malay beadwork and embroidery, in order to highlight some of the similarities and differences which distinguish the motifs, designs and workmanship, for Straits Chinese beadwork and embroidery – like many other arts and crafts of this genre – were influenced by Malay-Islamic culture.

I have, however, deliberately omitted to mention and describe beadwork of the peranakan communities in Indonesia, partly because my intention had been to concentrate purely on the antiquated arts and crafts peculiar to the Straits Chinese of the former Straits Settlements, and partly because I wanted to leave the discussion of Indonesian peranakan arts and crafts to other scholars who happen to have freer access to these artefacts, and who for this reason, have direct contacts with the remnants of Indonesian peranakans.

In order to appreciate works of art peculiar to a particular community one has to know the cultural ambience in which these artefacts were made. But a chance meeting last year with Mr Donald Harper, an American specialist in Indonesian batik, who now lives in Jogjakarta in Central Java, enabled me to view and examine some of these beadwork which, Mr Harper assured me, were procured from old peranakan homes in Java and Sumatra. Mr Harper travels extensively through Indonesia.

As it turned out, these samples of antiquated peranakan beadwork, mostly from Java and Sumatra, showed surprising similarities with those of Straits Chinese provenance in Malaysia and Singapore, not only in forms, but also in decorative motifs chosen.

The Indonesian nonyas used the same types of Rocaille and small metallic beads (apparently of nineteenth century French make) seen in Straits Chinese beadwork; and the techniques of working these beads were similar, namely, stringing, threading and stitching. Although Mr Harper made no mention of it, there is no doubt whatsoever, that as with similar artefacts found in old Straits Chinese homes, these articles were exclusively used during traditional wedding ceremonies.

There were no notable differences in materials, designs and techniques of craftsmanship other than variations in detail. Unless we were told to the contrary, any one of those beaded articles in Mr Harper's collection could have passed off as the handiwork of Straits nonyas – the difference in provenance would not have been apparent except to very trained eyes.

I have decided, therefore, to include this brief section on Indonesian peranakan beadwork, if for no better reason than to draw attention to the existence of these artefacts, and to provide, by way of the various illustrations, a basis for making a comparative study between these two geographically different, but culturally related, communities of overseas Chinese.

In their beadwork (and embroidery), as in everything else of peranakan origin, there were great affinities, as well as a strong sense of unity, between the language and culture of the Indonesian peranakan and the linguistic and cultural heritage of the Straits Chinese in Malaysia — geographical and other disparities notwithstanding. In the rest of this section, I shall highlight some of the salient features of Indonesian peranakan beadwork by selecting a few special items for analysis and description.

Some of the representative samples of old Indonesian peranakan beadwork which Mr Harper brought over to Singapore recently, consist of such articles as wedding purses made for attachment to ceremonial belts, ladies' wallets (or handbags), *sireh* leaf containers, rectangular table-mats apparently meant for blackwood (*Dalbergia*) table sets, belts, cigarette cases (called *daun nipah* for short), ornamental panels with long tassels meant for the bride's dressing mirror, wedding shoes and slippers, gold and silvergilt head ornaments for the bride's attendants, hanging ornaments (made in the round and in sets of three) for the wedding bed, square ceremonial containers (*tempat surat*) for holding the marriage contract (known as *surat kawin* in Malacca), door panels of silk embroidery ornamented with borders and tassels of beads, and some embroidered pillow ends known as *kepala bantal*.

Most of these items of extant Indonesian peranakan beadwork are also found in Straits Chinese beadwork. Two items, however, stand out as being peculiar to Indonesian peranakans: (1) the beaded cigarette case known simply as *daun nipah*, and (2) the square document case presumably intended for holding the marriage contract, and thus known as *tempat surat*.

I did not find among the various items in Mr Harper's collection of antique Indonesian peranakan beadwork, such articles as embroidered-cum-beaded skull caps (two types) used by the babas in Malacca, *sapu tangan* panels, *selendang* (ornamental shoulder drapes for the bride), spectacle cases, knee-cap ornaments, bed-runners, comb boxes, *bantal* panels fabricated entirely out of stitched Rocaille beads, beaded panels for ceremonial trays, bridal stools, food covers, candles, etc.

One may presume nonetheless that such items of beadwork must also have been used by Indonesian peranakans in their wedding ceremonies in the days gone by, but that many of these artefacts could have been irreparably damaged or lost through wear and tear, or else destroyed in the depredations which came in the wake of World War II and civil wars in Indonesia before and after Independence in 1949.

Daun nipah cigarette case

The *daun nipah* cigarette case consists of two separate, flattened U-shaped pouches, each of which is open at one end (see figs. 40, 41). One of these U-shaped pouches is somewhat shorter in length but broader in width than the other. The shorter pouch is intended to serve as a cover, and it is just wide enough to enable the slimmer and longer pouch to fit snugly into its open end. This slimmer pouch was meant to hold thin, rolled strips of dry *nipah* leaves, which served as tobacco wrappers for making hand-rolled cigarettes. The tobacco was usually carried in a separate silver container known as *chelpa*.

Fig. 40 Three examples of the elegant *daun nipah* cigarette cases made specially for the groom. The custom of smoking home-made cigarettes wrapped with dried *nipah* leaves was adapted from the Javanese. In the hands of the artistic Indonesian nonyas, the humble cigarette case was turned into a thing of beauty. Collection of Donald Harper.

The custom of smoking *rokok daun nipah* or *tembakau*, as this type of cigarette is known to Singapore Malays, was probably more prevalent among traditional Indonesian peranakans than their Straits Chinese counterparts in Singapore, Malacca and Penang. My own impression is that the traditional Straits Chinese of Malacca preferred chewing *sireh* leaves to smoking, whether the Western imported type of Virginia cigarettes or *tembakau*.

In any case, my own childhood recollection of *rokok daun nipah* or *tembakau* was that when lighted, both the *nipah* leaf wrappers and the local variety of tobacco gave off a most acrid and unpleasant smell, so much so that my mother had to discourage my father from smoking *tembakau* at home. *Tembakau* was rarely used by Singaporean

Straits Chinese. The nonyas, of course, did not smoke, because it was traditionally considered bad etiquette for women to smoke.

But while the acrid smell was offensive, those beaded, *daun nipah* cigarette cases were often beautifully crafted. They are usually fabricated out of purple, maroon or green velvet, stiffened with cotton and paper, and then ornamented with small, coloured Rocaille beads of about 1 mm in diameter, closely stitched together to form colourful designs of floral and foliated motifs, either with or without insects (e.g. butterflies and crickets), birds (e.g. quails, mandarin ducks, storks, cranes), and mythical beasts (e.g. *qilins*, dragons and phoenixes) – auspicious symbols all derived from ancient Chinese art motifs.

Sometimes small faceted metallic beads, only about 0.5 mm in diameter, are employed in combination with Rocaille glass beads for depicting these decorative motifs, and the tiny facetings on these metallic beads give these cases a jewellike touch of luxury when they glimmer in the light.

The traditional nonyas of Indonesia who fabricated these *daun nipah* cigarette cases – and it may be presumed that most of these beaded artefacts were the handiwork of the nonyas – even took the trouble to decorate the tops and bottoms of these U-shaped cases with beaded ornaments, painstakingly stitched into position.

Such cigarette cases are, of course, rarely seen in old family heirlooms of Straits Chinese homes. In

Fig. 41 Two more examples of *daun nipah* cigarette cases. The external surfaces of these cases are densely stitched with an opaque type of Rocaille beads. One of them is even 'inscribed' with the name of the original owner. From Java? Probably of early twentieth century dating. Collection of Donald Harper.

Mrs Grace Saw's collection of magnificent bead-work and embroidery, mostly procured from Straits Chinese homes and antique dealers in Penang, there is one such *daun nipah* cigarette case which she and most antique collectors mistakenly described as a 'spectacle case'; and until Mr Harper drew my attention to the fact that in Indonesian peranakan communities such articles were regularly used as cigarette cases, I would have thought that they were indeed spectacle cases.

However, this Penang version of the *daun nipah* case is so similar to the Indonesian variety seen in Harper's collection, that one can safely presume that it was modelled on the Indonesian archetype found in Semarang, Batavia and Medan where, before the War, sizeable communities of Indonesian peranakans once had their homes. It is even possible that Mrs Saw's 'spectacle case' was made in Medan and then brought over to Georgetown, Penang, at the turn of the present century.

Tempat surat

The next beaded item which I have not encountered before in all these sixteen years of handling and studying Straits Chinese antiques, is the document case known in Indonesian peranakan usage as *tempat surat* – literally, 'a letter case' or 'letter container'.

Mr Harper said that all his Indonesian peranakans merely described this flattened, square, bead-embroidered case as *tempat surat*. But since most of these beaded articles, like their counterparts found in old Straits Chinese homes in Malaysia, were used only for wedding ceremonies, the so-called *tempat surat* was no ordinary letter case, like the postman's brown canvas letter bag: it was, in fact, a document case for holding the traditional peranakan wedding contract (see figs. 42 & 43).

In old Malacca Straits Chinese customs, the wedding contract was known as *surat kawin*, or

Fig. 42 *Tempat surat* is a square bead-embroidered container somewhat shaped like an envelope, and used in both Straits Chinese and Indonesian peranakan communities for the ceremonial presentation of the wedding contract or certificate. This particular example comes from a peranakan family in Java. The *tempat surat* is hardly seen in Malacca, Penang or even Singapore Straits Chinese heirlooms. Dimensions: approximately 20 cm square. Probably late nineteenth or early twentieth century dating. Collection of Donald Harper.

literally, 'letter of marriage'. But for some reason or other, I have never heard it mentioned before that a specially embroidered or beaded document case made to contain the traditional wedding contract, was customarily used in Straits Chinese wedding ceremonies in Malaya.

Over the years, I have been fortunate enough to have gained access to the private collections of some prominent collectors of Straits Chinese beadwork and embroidery, but never once had I encountered any object remotely resembling the *tempat surat* which Mr Harper brought to Singapore for us to examine. How, it may be asked, was

Fig. 43 Another example of Indonesian peranakan *tempat surat* showing both the obverse and reverse sides ornamented with designs of *qilin* and floral motifs stitched out of Rocaille beads against a maroon velvet backing. Dimensions: 20 cm square. Probably of late nineteenth or early twentieth century dating. From Java. Collection of Donald Harper.

the *surat kawin* of the traditional Straits Chinese of Malacca, Penang and Singapore, presented by the bridegroom's family to the bride's parents?

More likely than not, the *surat kawin* was wrapped in a large square piece of damask silk (either red or pink was considered auspicious) resembling a large handkerchief and then placed in a brass, silver or better still, red lacquer tray, and then ceremoniously carried by the groom's attendants to the bride's parental home, somewhat after the manner of the Minangkabau Malays of Negri Sembilan.

In any case, the *tempat surat* in extant today (and I date the four or five-odd samples in Mr Harper's collection to early twentieth century purely on stylistic grounds) is fabricated out of a square panel of velvet, stiffened as usual with cotton and paper backings, after the beaded designs have been stitched on to the velvet surface.

The stitching of the small, coloured Rocaille beads was facilitated by the traditional embroidery frame or *pidangan*. Panels of this type usually measure 20 cm square.

When all the four edges along the panel have been securely hemmed to prevent fraying, the panel is folded inward until all the triangular sides of the four corners meet. The reduced square panel

Fig. 44 Ceremonial wedding purses (two of which are incomplete) meant to be attached to matching bead-embroidered belts shown here, are typical of Straits Chinese purses, though these specimens came from Indonesia. The Straits Chinese as well as their Indonesian counterparts, loved bright and contrasting colours, and these purses are among the more colourful ones seen in Straits Chinese family heirlooms. Collection of Donald Harper.

now measures approximately 20 cm square. The sides or edges of the three corner foldings are now stitched together, leaving one corner flap free and open like the cover of an envelope.

A decorated beaded strap about 1.7 cm wide and 30 cm long is now attached to the pointed end of the flap. This strip is lengthened by the addition of a plain silk strip 40 cm long. The extended silk strap enables the *tempat surat* to be securely tied together.

The decorative designs on the cover of the *tempat surat* are usually arranged to fit the square format of the marriage document case, and the motifs employed are, as in all traditional Chinese decorative arts, selected to fit the purpose or occasion for which it is used.

For the *tempat surat*, the standard motifs are either a pair of phoenixes or else a pair of dragons, combined with peony blossoms. Sometimes butterflies, magpies, quails and storks (always employed in pairs) are added to make the design appear more ornate, for the Straits Chinese and their Indonesian peranakan compatriots were fond of ornate designs.

While red was traditionally regarded as the most auspicious colour for all important ceremonial occasions in China, most of the extant beaded articles made by the Malayan and Indonesian nonyas were stitched on purple velvet. Thus, their purses, handbags, belts, panels, table-mats, cigarette cases, ceremonial caps, collar panels, etc., were made from purple velvet.

Fig. 45 Four specimens of ladies' wallets used specifically during peranakan as well as Straits Chinese/traditional wedding ceremonies. Notice that they come in different sizes, and those from Indonesia appear to have been exclusively fabricated on maroon velvet backings. The ornamental designs, all executed in stitched Rocaille beads, were common to Straits Chinese culture. All such wallets (meant to be carried in the hand) were made out of one piece of embroidered panel and folded into three panels to form the wallet. The largest of these wallets is 5½ inches long and 4 inches wide. Collection of Donald Harper.

Why purple should have been preferred to red is not entirely clear to me, because scarlet red and tomato red velvets were readily available and used from time to time – albeit only for border decorations. One can only speculate, in the absence of more reliable information, that some Malayan babas and/or some Indonesian peranakans, some time during the nineteenth century, had fortuitously hit upon the idea that purple, because of its richer and deeper hue, could perhaps serve as a good substitute for red, and what started out as a quirk, soon became an established custom with the passage of time.

Purses and wallets

There are two types of extant purses in Straits Chinese and Indonesian peranakan beadwork. The first type resembles a modified pocket (see figs. 25 & 44) and always comes with an upper appendage

Fig. 46 Another example of a wedding wallet from Indonesia. Notice that the principal motifs consist of the *qilin*, a pair of phoenixes and a cockerel. According to my information, wallets with more 'masculine' motifs were intended for the groom, while those with more 'feminine' motifs (e.g. flowers, butterflies) were meant for the bride. It is possible that this custom was peculiar to the peranakan Chinese in Indonesia. Collection of Donald Harper.

made of cotton and flannel fabric. This upper appendage is to enable the purse to be slipped into the ceremonial wedding belt.

Purses intended for the groom are slightly larger than those intended for the bride. But the distinction can also be detected in the kinds of decorative motifs employed: dragons and *qilins*, for example, were invariably meant for the groom's purse, while peonies and phoenixes were considered more appropriately feminine in taste.

A typical groom's purse is about 14 cm long and 10 cm wide, while the bride's purse is 12 to 12.5 cm long and 9 cm wide. Rocaille and small, faceted metallic beads between 0.5 and 1 mm in diameter were commonly employed. These beads are, almost without exception, stitched on to purple or blue-green velvet, stiffened as usual with red cotton backing.

The second type of purses, or rather, wallets intended for ladies, is of a somewhat different design (see figs. 45 & 46). Basically, it consists of a rectangular panel of purple (or sometimes emerald green) velvet 24 cm long and 14.5 cm wide, and stiffened with scarlet red cotton backing.

This rectangular panel is then folded inward three times – the first two foldings being fabricated into two separate flaps for containing currency notes, while the third folding is cut into the shape of a semi-circular or U-shaped flap, to serve as a cover for the completed wallet. This flap is usually securely held down by an ornamental button and a black cotton loop.

But before the rectangular velvet panel is folded to form the wallet, it has to be ornamented with beaded designs. This is effected by tracing white markings on the frontal surface of the velvet depicting the standard decorative motifs traditionally regarded as appropriate for wedding artefacts, namely, dragons, *qilins*, phoenixes, peonies, quails, butterflies, storks or floral sprigs derived from the flowers of the four seasons. Once the tracings have been completed, the velvet panel is stretched tightly on to the traditional embroidery frame, and Rocaille beads are then painstakingly stitched on to the spaces enclosed by the decorative motifs.

These rectangular wallets are small enough to be held comfortably in the palm of one's hand.

Fig. 47 This pair of embroidered *bantal* panels is less abstract in its designs – the fish and flower motifs, although rather formalized, are nonetheless recognizable as such. The key fret border designs in gold thread couchings betray their Chinese origins. However, the embroidery on the scarlet background is entirely composed of cross-stitches: Chinese embroiderers rarely used the cross-stitch except for ornamental details. Collection of Donald Harper.

Bantal panels

Some comments on *bantal* (pillow and bolster) panels are in order here, even though they are not beaded articles but cotton and cotton gauze panels embroidered in silk, woollen and gold threads. This is because the Indonesian peranakan variety is distinctively unusual compared to *bantal* panels used by the traditional Straits Chinese.

As I have discussed in some detail in another work of mine,[13] pillow and bolster ends made to Straits Chinese taste were fabricated out of rectangular, circular and octagonal plates of silver; while their decorative designs were largely culled from the vast repertoire of traditional Chinese art and religious symbols.

The techniques of chased and repoussé work

were employed to depict the various motifs on these silver plates. By and large, the dimensions of those rectangular *bantal* plates vary between 11 cm by 6.5 cm and 15 cm by 9 cm for the larger pieces; while those for bolster ends, if they happen to be circular, average 10 cm in diameter. Those with an octagonal shape have a width averaging 11 cm.

Straits Chinese *bantal* panels fabricated out of velvet panels and stitched with Rocaille beads are few and far between. They are smaller in size, and in the days gone by, were probably used only by the lower-income Straits Chinese families. Otherwise, *bantal* plates were generally made of silver, and in rare cases, of gold plates. For this reason, *bantal* panels executed out of embroidered beads or silk and gold threads, are rarely seen in Singapore, Malacca and Penang.

Fig. 48 The design on this simple but pleasing, silk embroidered *bantal* panel (one of a pair) is unique as it is imaginative: it utilizes only one type of stitches, namely, the alternating satin stitch. And yet by the skilful choice of colours and patterns, the nameless embroiderer was able to turn out a thing of beauty. Collection of Donald Harper.

This is apparently not the case with Indonesian peranakan *bantal* plates, if the eight sets of *bantal* panels Mr Harper brought to Singapore can be regarded as sufficiently representative. Indeed, Indonesian peranakan *bantal* plates are neither fabricated out of silver plates nor Rocaille beads and velvet fabrics: they all appear to be embroidered with silk, gold threads and even woollen threads (see fig. 47).

What is more, the designs consist entirely of geometric patterns such as zig-zag lines, squares, diamond patterns, triangles, rectangles and key-fret patterns, after the designs of various native tribes in Indonesia, such as the Sumba and Flores tribes, the Bataks of Sumatra and the Todrajans of Sulawesi. The shades of brown, blue and red used are simple and very attractive. So, too, are the kinds of stitches employed: only one kind of stitch was used in embroidering all the various geometric designs in a particular set of *bantal* panels. For example, if the embroiderer had decided on using cross-stitch, then all the motifs will be embroidered by the use of the cross-stitch; if the *petit point* stitch was preferred, then it would be used

throughout. In particular, the use of the short, alternating satin stitch produced *bantal* panels of a most pleasing design and texture (see fig. 48).

Why Indonesian nonyas should have abandoned the use of traditional Chinese motifs for the decorative designs of these *bantal* panels, preferring instead the exclusive use of geometric patterns favoured by native tribes, is not at all clear to me. For in all other artefacts (beaded or embroidered) used in traditional peranakan ceremonies, they adhered closely to Chinese art and religious symbols.

Why were the patterns and designs of *bantal* panels excepted? There were no bolster panels in Mr Harper's collection: I would have liked to find out if these panels also carried exclusively geometric patterns. Perhaps these *bantal* panels were intended for Indonesian rather than peranakan Chinese clients? Obviously, more research has to be done on this matter.

Indonesian *bantal* panels are significantly larger than their counterparts in the Straits Settlements: a typical pillow panel measures 17.5 cm by 10.5 cm.

PART II

STRAITS CHINESE EMBROIDERY

8
The Art of Painting
with a Needle

EMBROIDERY IS THE art of creating artistic designs on woven fabric by the use of needles and threads. While this may sound somewhat trite as a definition, the art of embroidery itself has always evoked much praise and admiration throughout the ages, by the sheer artistry of its designs, the variety and splendour of its colours and the cunning ingenuity of its stitchery.

It is, in fact, an art of great antiquity going back several thousand years to the ancient civilizations of Egypt, Mesopotamia, Persia and China. For this reason, perhaps, the basic tools required for stitching are of extreme simplicity, namely, an iron needle, several lengths of coloured threads and a piece of woven fabric. But the remarkable thing about embroidery is that the unsophisticated nature of its working implements has never been an obstacle in preventing skilled and imaginative embroiderers from turning out needlework of ingenious designs and surpassing beauty.

The ancient Romans were particularly enthusiastic in their admiration and appreciation of the painterly qualities of embroidery, especially embroidery done on Chinese silk, then a commodity of the greatest luxury. The famous poet, Virgil (70–19 B.C.), or Publius Vergilius Maro, to give his full name, was moved to use the infinitive of the Latin word, 'to paint', namely, *pingere*, to describe embroidery. This Virgilian licence became a permanent feature of the Latin vocabulary; as the

Latin word for 'embroidery' is, in fact, *arcu pingere*, while its more formal phrasing is *ars arcu pingendi* – in other words, 'the art of painting with a needle'.

Chinese embroidery

The Chinese, however, were the first people in the world to discover the art of reeling off silk threads directly from the cocoon of the silkworm belonging to the species of moths, *Bombyx mori*, without having to pluck the cocoons into small fluffy pieces for spinning into coarse silk threads.

Indeed, the art of spinning threads from the cocoons of wild silk moths was known in India, Assyria, Persia and some other parts of the Middle East as far back as 2000 B.C. But the art of unwinding the silken skein directly from the cocoon was exclusively an invention of the Chinese probably dating back to about the beginning of the Zhou dynasty (1122–255 B.C.).

In Chinese, embroidery is described as *cixiu* (刺绣) or *huixiu* (绘绣), while the embroiderer is known as *guxiu shifu* (顾绣师传). And incidentally, the Latin word for silk, namely, *seres*, and the English word 'silk', are both derived from the Chinese word of almost the same sound, *si*. Even the Malay word for silk, *sutra*, and embroidery, *sulam*, have the same phoneme as *si*.

90

In traditional China, however, embroidery was regarded as a minor art, even though the garments and robes fabricated by the humble and anonymous embroiderer were sufficiently important to be worn by the Emperor, the Royal Family and the nobility on important state ceremonies. Indeed, the dragon robes stitched by Chinese embroiderers are among the most splendid embroideries in the world.

Straits Chinese embroidery

Straits Chinese embroidery belongs to the same tradition of needlework in China, in the sense that the materials were peculiarly Chinese in origin, these being silk threads and silk fabrics, the motifs of the decorative designs and the techniques of stitchery employed. But the needlework stitched by the nonyas themselves, as well as those embroidered artefacts made to Straits Chinese specifications, differed in some significant respects from the handiwork of professional embroiderers in China.

Until now, a detailed study of Straits Chinese embroidery has not been attempted, even though its existence has been known to most students of Straits Chinese culture for a long time. However, Straits Chinese embroidery, the actual handiwork of a bygone generation of nonyas, has become a lost art. There is no possibility that the nonyas will ever again revive this graceful pastime. Hence, this essay has been written with the aim of setting down on record a description of what remains of these highly perishable artefacts, and to capture in pictures the unique characteristics of their craftsmanship, before they disappear altogether. This essay is also intended to be an appreciation of a vanished and fascinating art.

Of the distinctive cultural artefacts peculiar to the Straits Chinese community, beadwork and embroidery may be regarded as the true and authentic handicrafts of the Straits Chinese themselves. The rest of these cultural objects which were traditionally associated with the Straits Chinese way of life, namely, their gold and silverware, distinctive porcelain ware, costumes, furniture, and architecture – were made by artisans and craftsmen of non-Straits Chinese extraction to their requirements and specifications.

This is not particularly surprising because we know for a fact that the Straits Chinese disliked professions which entailed much sweat and manual labour, for example, carpentry, pottery, farming and building construction. They preferred the professions of traders, merchants, doctors and lawyers, and the majority were clerical workers in the Colonial Civil Service.

As strict adherents to Confucianism, their menfolk tended to despise manual work, especially work of a menial sort. So, although beadwork and embroidery were largely the handicrafts of the Straits Chinese community, they were in fact created by the nonyas.

However, in attributing Straits Chinese beadwork and embroidery to the skilled and patient handicrafts of a bygone generation of nonyas, we have to add a note of caution here. By and large, this assumption is true when applied to most extant pieces of old *beadwork*. But when it comes to *embroidery*, we encounter some difficulty.

Many extant pieces of old embroidery found in traditional Straits Chinese homes have turned out to have been the handiwork of embroiderers from Canton, Fujian and Zhejiang rather than that of the nonyas – as some elderly nonyas will tell you (see fig. 49).

The problem of identification is further complicated by the fact that traditional embroideries, like all the so-called 'minor arts' of Chinese origin, did not bear the names or signatures of their artisans, nor the dates and places of manufacture. And in any case, as most of the older nonyas were

Fig. 49 Embroidered altar cloth for square altar-table. This rich and gorgeously embroidered altar hanging, 3 feet by 3 feet, was obviously intended for Chinese as well as Straits Chinese wedding ceremonies. Notice the prominently featured pair of phoenixes, a pair of quails, a cock and a hen, magpies, and what looks like peacocks. The impressive peonies worked in relief gold threads are, of course, traditionally associated with weddings. However, large embroidered panels of this type were very rarely fabricated by the Straits nonyas. This one was probably made by embroiderers from Fujian. Late nineteenth century. Collection of Mrs Ho Wing Meng.

illiterate, they did not attach names to their own handiwork.

Besides, the local nonyas and their counterparts in China were trained in the same tradition of needlework; they employed the same techniques of stitching, kinds of stitches employed, materials, equipment and motifs of the decorative designs utilized. Indeed, in the eyes of most people, there are no palpable differences between nonya embroideries and those of Chinese origin – not, that is, until one looks hard and long enough (see fig. 50).

Generally speaking, nonya workmanship is characterized by the *smaller* pieces of embroidery in

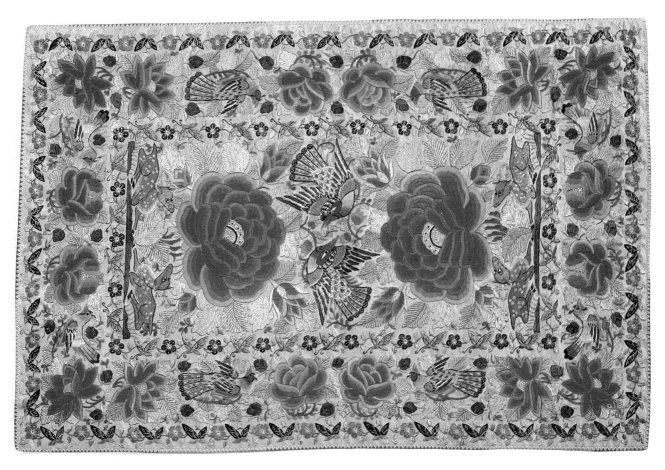

Fig. 50 Embroidered rectangular panel probably intended for a blackwood (*Dalbergia*) tea-table which usually comes with a pair of square, throne-like blackwood armchairs placed on either side. Incidentally, green was a favourite colour among the Straits Chinese in Peninsular Malaya. The motifs depicted here were largely considered auspicious for a traditional Chinese wedding, namely, peonies, a pair of phoenixes, butterflies, deer and magpies. Notice that the peonies shown here look more like roses – a characteristic of Penang workmanship. Length: 13 inches. Width: 8½ inches. Probably late nineteenth/early twentieth century. From Penang. Collection of Mrs Ho Wing Meng.

extant, namely, pillow and bolster cases, small rectangular panels for tea-tables, ornamental hangings (the so-called 'gewgaws') for the wedding bed and the wash-stand, panels for purses, *sapu tangan*, *selendang*, spectacle cases, *sireh* boxes, ceremonial trays, candle-covers, toe-covers on slippers, etc., which, by universal consent of people in the Straits Chinese community, were said to have been made by a bygone generation of nonyas.

This is not always so, as there are quite a number of small embroidered items which, on stylistic considerations, could not have been of nonya workmanship. For example, the pair of crescent-shaped panels embroidered on a background of yellow silk in fig. 51, and which was intended for the toe-coverings of wedding slippers is most probably the work of some skilled embroiderer in China, and not that of some Straits nonya.

All the decorative motifs here are executed by using one type of stitch only, namely, the chain stitch. But notice how very minute each of these stitches is – 0.5 mm in fact. In order to fill one square inch of space with these tiny embroidered chain stitches, one actually requires 50 x 50 stitches or a total of 2,500 knots in all! The stitches are so minute and closely packed together, that I had to use an X10 magnification hand-lens to make out the structure of each of those looped stitches.

We know that the unknown embroiderer used a needle of extreme fineness and silk threads of spidery thinness to execute those stitches. But

Fig. 51 Samples of crescent-shaped covering for wedding slippers showing the various stages involved in their craftsmanship. The topmost panels set against a yellow silk background were probably not the works of Straits nonyas, because the fine decorative designs were all executed in minute chain stitches, each of which is less than 0.5 mm across. Straits nonyas seldom worked with chain stitches, except for ornamental details. Properties of Mr Peter Wee and Mrs Ho Wing Meng.

how, one wonders, did she contrive to manipulate thread and needle for executing such tiny chain loops without the aid of a magnifying glass? Even assuming that the unknown but talented embroiderer had exceptionally acute vision, the execution of such infinitesimal stitches is bound to cause severe eye-strain within a very short time.

Even under the most favourable conditions stitching of this sort must necessarily be a slow and tedious process; so how long did it take to embroider those thousands of stitches (and there must be close to 10,000 stitches in one of these panels) to complete a pair of these slipper-panels?

There is a popular legend among students of traditional Chinese embroidery which is repeated in Alan Priest's and Pauline Simon's book, *Chinese Textiles*, Metropolitan Museum Exhibition, N.Y. 1931–32, that the Peking knot (commonly seen on many late nineteenth century embroidered panels found in old Straits Chinese homes) was so incredibly difficult to execute that it became known as 'the forbidden knot', 'because so many women were going blind doing this knot, so that the Chinese government had to stop its use.'[14]

Mr Priest did not, however, say whether this story about women embroiderers going blind as a result of stitching Peking knots was in fact true, or just hearsay. Nor did he say when, if ever, the Imperial government in Peking passed a law to prohibit its use in embroidery. One presumes that the law was promulgated some time during the nineteenth century. But even so, many extant pieces of Chinese embroidery found in old Straits Chinese homes may be dated to the first two decades of the present century; and they were still largely embroidered in Peking knots!

The story must be taken with a pinch of salt. Actually, there are two kinds of Peking knots: one is the so-called 'Pekinese stitch' which is in fact a combination of back stitches interlaced with a series of loops (see diagram below). The other is the 'seed stitch' which is very similar to the French knot, and is executed by making several turns of the thread round the needle and stitching the resultant knot into the fabric (see diagram overleaf).

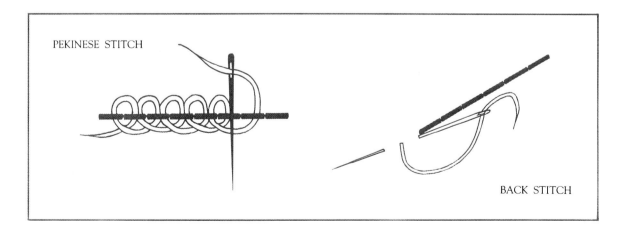

PEKINESE STITCH

BACK STITCH

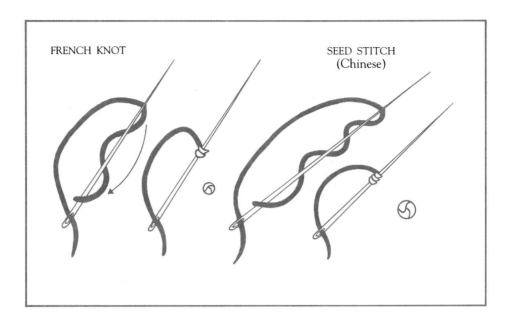

FRENCH KNOT

SEED STITCH
(Chinese)

The stitching of either of these 'knots' does not pose insuperable difficulty – not, that is, in the dexterous hands of a practised embroiderer. And the proof of this is that many extant pieces of old embroideries are filled with the Pekinese stitch.

Besides, a study of the various samples of Peking knots used in Chinese embroideries shows that the Pekinese knot (or loop to be more precise) varies between 1 and 1½ mm in size. Similarly, an examination of those embroideries using the seed stitch shows that the size of the knots varies between 1 and 2 mm.

All such knots are clearly and distinctly visible to the naked eye, and can hence be easily executed. Since French embroiderers have no legends about their own kinds suffering blindness as a result of stitching French knots, I cannot see how their counterparts in China could have suffered irreparable damage to their own eyes by working at the Pekinese stitch or the seed stitch.

Nonetheless, the story about the evil reputation of the 'forbidden knot' was not entirely spurious. There is obviously some basis to it although, in my opinion, it was not the *stitching* of either the Peking stitch or seed knot as such, but rather *the attempt to miniaturize the technique of executing these knots to the limits of the embroiderer's skill*, which put such an intolerable strain upon one's eyes.

Thus any embroiderer who attempts to make a living by demonstrating his or her skill at produc-

ing stitches similar to those shown on the four panels in fig. 52 – these being tiny Pekinese stitches no bigger than 0.5 mm in size – had better consider retiring within five years, or else risk the prospect of permanently damaged vision.

In executing knots of such critical dimensions, even embroiderers with perfect vision and exceptionally nimble fingers will feel the strain of total concentration after a short period of work. And considering that each of these panels measuring no more than 8 inches by 2½ inches, has crammed within them, an average of between 25,000 and 30,000 stitches, one can appreciate the prodigious labour and patience required, just to complete one of these panels.

Since labour was cheap in old China, even the most skilful of craftsmen had to toil hard and long just to earn a mere pittance. Hence, if some poverty-stricken embroiderers, malnourished and overworked, succumbed to blindness after years of labouring at these incredibly small and difficult stitches, we can well sympathize with the report about the Chinese government's decision to ban the use of such stitches in embroidery.

Fortunately for the Straits nonyas, the various problems associated with the stitching of the Pekinese stitch, the seed knot and the chain stitch did not arise, because these stitches were seldom used exclusively in Straits Chinese embroidery. Authentic nonya embroidered works were, more

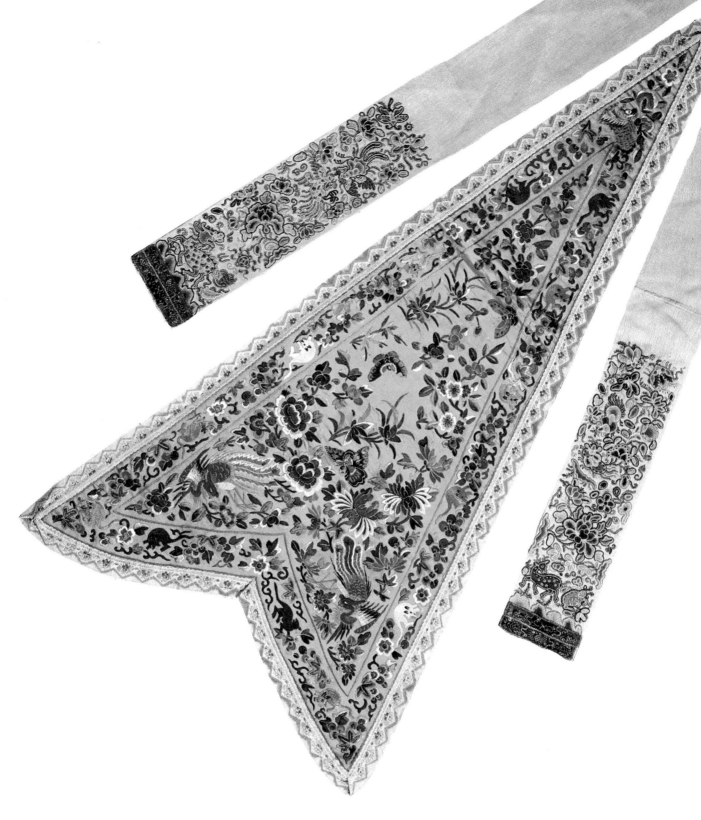

Fig. 52 The triangular-like, yellow embroidered panel shown here, is a bridal *selendang* which formerly belonged to a wealthy Straits Chinese family in Singapore. The small but crowded designs are finely worked in satin stitches. The two pale green embroidered panels are actually parts of a silk belt intended for a traditional bridegroom. The significant feature of the embroidery is the use of extremely fine Pekinese knots for all the decorative motifs. It is estimated that there are more than 25,000 stitches on each of these embroidered panels – and there are four such panels on this belt! Late nineteenth/early twentieth century. Collection of Mrs Grace Saw.

Fig. 53 Embroidered, rectangular silk panel with designs of peonies and a pair of phoenixes enclosed by a green border embellished with tiny figures of stags and floral and foliated motifs. What is remarkable about the ornamental design is that it is entirely executed with fine chain stitches, each loop no larger than 0.5 mm in diameter. Probably not of Straits Chinese workmanship. Length: 18 inches. Width: 10 inches. Author's collection.

often than not, executed largely in satin stitches, wtih stem stitches, Pekinese stitches, seed stitches, superimposed stitches of several varieties and couchings used only for filling in the details. Hence, those small embroidered panels fabricated out of minute chain stitches, seed knots or Pekinese stitches may, in most instances, be attributed to the workmanship of native Chinese embroiderers (see fig. 53).

Nonetheless, I have, on occasion, come across some Penang-styled embroideries stitched largely with the Pekinese stitch, and I was told, contrary to my expectation, that they were made by a former generation of Penang nonyas. This is entirely possible, except that by and large, the nonyas preferred the rich and more painterly effects of the satin stitch and its several variations (see fig. 54).

On the other hand, professional embroiderers in China were probably better trained to execute a wider variety of stitches. They also enjoyed the patronage of the Court and the nobility who, naturally, demanded the highest standard of ex-

cellence in the art of stitchery. No such professionalism was required of the Straits nonyas. Theirs was at best, an amateur pastime for which they received only informal training from their mothers and other elderly female relatives.

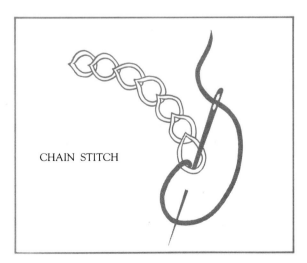

CHAIN STITCH

Fig. 54 This is a representative example of traditional Straits Chinese embroidery executed entirely out of fine satin stitches; seed stitches and stem stitches were used only for the minor details. The design is predominantly of peony blossoms in blue, purple, rose-pink and yellow complemented by birds and butterflies, all of which were traditionally propitious for wedding ceremonies. This embroidered panel was probably used as an ornamental cover for the blackwood tea-table. Length: 14 inches. Width: 10 inches. Probably of late nineteenth or early twentieth century dating. From Penang. Collection of Mrs Ho Wing Meng.

The Art of Painting with a Needle 99

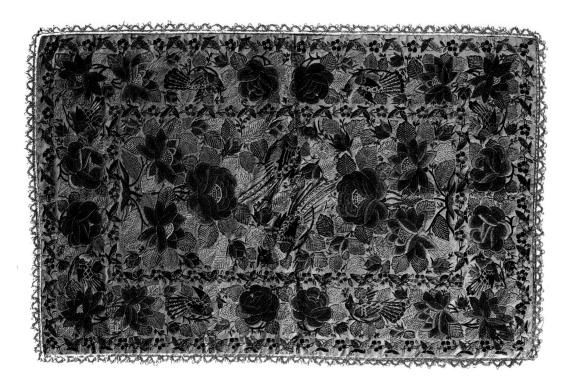

Fig. 55 Another embroidered silk panel typical of Straits Chinese embroidery: the floral and foliated motifs, mainly of red and purple peonies, with a pair of phoenixes and peacock-like birds, are densely packed into the space provided. It is, in fact, a paradigm example of Penang workmanship. Probably late nineteenth/early twentieth century. Collection of Mrs Grace Saw.

But in a piece of embroidery of nonya workmanship one rarely comes across motifs of pure Chinese taste, namely, dragons, *qilins*, Buddhist lions, figures in landscape or architectural settings, figures of lohans and other Taoist immortals, pine trees, bamboos, chrysanthemums, prunus, magnolias, gardenia, wisteria, fishes, crabs, prawns, storks, cranes, tigers, etc. One may, of course, see such motifs in large embroidered panels made by Chinese embroiderers for use in Straits Chinese homes.

Likewise, those ready-made pieces bought from local embroidery shops and haberdashers were bound to be more traditionally Chinese in taste, not only from the kinds of motifs generally preferred, but also in the techniques of stitchery employed. Imported embroideries often came with the Peking stitch, the seed knot, the chain stitch, or else a combination of the satin stitch with extensive couchings of gold and silver threads.

In the days gone by, most young nonyas were taught the art of embroidery as a necessary duty; for every potential bride was expected to sew and decorate her own pillow and bolster cases, bridal slippers and other odds and ends, with embroidered patterns. At no time was embroidery undertaken for the sake of making a living. Hence, the rigorous training and experience required of professional embroiderers in China were not applicable to home-bred embroiderers.

A typical piece of Straits Chinese embroidery is usually of rather modest proportions, perhaps no bigger than a standard-sized pillow-case. As with designs on porcelain ware made to their specifications,[15] the motifs employed are largely of the floral and foliated variety (the tree-peony with large blossoms being generally preferred to other flowers), and those together with a pair of phoenixes, form the standard theme of nonya design. Occasionally, butterflies, lotus blossoms, goldfish, squirrels, cocks and hens and mandarin ducks are included (see fig. 55).

9
Techniques of Embroidery

Painterly stitchwork

MOST EXTANT PIECES of nonya embroidery were fabricated by the use of one principal type of stitching, namely, the 'satin stitch' and variations of it including long and short stitches, overlapping stitches or alternate stitches.

Basically, the satin stitch consists of a series of closely-laid, parallel stitches used for filling up a decorative pattern. Satin stitches can be varied in a number of different ways, such as alternate long and short stitches, overlapping stitches superimposed one upon another, or several rows of short parallel stitches arranged in staggered fashion.

The satin stitch and its variations are familiar to embroiderers of every culture all over the world, so on the face of it, there was nothing remarkable about the fact that many old Chinese embroideries, and *practically all* nonya embroideries, were executed with this familiar stitch. And yet when Chinese embroidery first arrived in Europe during the late seventeenth century and was shown to select groups of people among the nobility, it elicited enthusiastic admiration among those who were privileged to view these exotic works of stitchery.

What was there in these embroidered panels and drapes which caused such a sensation with the Europeans? Several features of traditional Chinese embroideries were new and fascinating in European eyes.

First of all, Chinese embroideries were, without exception, *silk-on-silk* embroideries. In other words, threads and fabrics were all made of silk – something rarely seen in Europe, except perhaps in the sumptuous costumes worn by the bishops and high dignitaries of the Eastern Orthodox Churches as far back as the seventh century A.D.

European embroideries, by contrast, were largely of wool-on-canvas, wool-on-linen or wool-on-

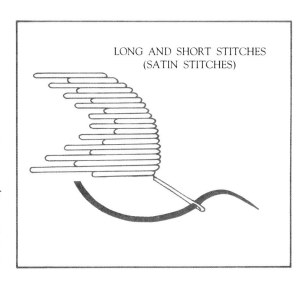

LONG AND SHORT STITCHES
(SATIN STITCHES)

flaxen fabrics; and since woollen threads were coarser and more hairy in texture, embroideries fabricated out of such threads did not impart the same kind of sheen, colour and delicacy which silk-on-silk embroideries displayed so richly.

When they first appeared in Europe, Chinese embroideries had all the exotic beauty and mystery which Europeans always associated with China and the Far East. The motifs found on their designs were, if anything, strange and attractive. For example, the dragon which in the West was traditionally associated with Satan himself, and the forces of evil, was here depicted with all the power and grandeur befitting an imperial insignia.

The *qilin*, the Buddhist lion and the phoenix were exotic enough to remind one of animals which appear only in fairy tales. As for splendidly garbed Oriental figures seen in Court settings and against very quaint-looking buildings never encountered in Europe, these only aroused more speculations about the fabulous riches of the East.[16]

But what really stole the unstinted admiration of Western embroiderers was the ability of their Oriental counterparts to depict flowers, foliage, birds and insects with spontaneity, a sureness of touch and a vivid sense of realism unequalled by anything which Europeans had ever managed with needle and thread. For there, emblazoned on those delicate and shimmering fabrics, were 'paintings' of magnificent peonies, chrysanthemums, prunus, lotuses, magnolias, camellias, gardenias, wisteria, gnarled and twisted pine trees, birds of exotic shapes and colours, lovely mandarin ducks, pirouetting storks and cranes, butterflies and leaping carps, all vividly portrayed as if they had an inner life and vitality of their own (see fig. 57).

As European embroiderers came to discover, upon studying Chinese embroidery closely, what made Chinese embroidery so fascinating and refreshing in their eyes – apart from the loveliness of the materials they employed, namely, silk-on-silk, and their exotic decorative motifs – was the technique of stitchery peculiar to their tradition.

By this I do not mean the types of stitches the Chinese generally employed; for most of them in any case, were familiar to other embroiderers outside China. It is true that the Chinese exploited the techniques of chain stitching and seed-knot stitching (see figs. 51, 52 & 57) to their utmost limits of miniaturization. Few embroiderers ever matched them in the execution of loops and knots no bigger than 0.5 mm in diameter; and there must be very few embroiderers elsewhere in the world who could cram as many as 2,500 stitches into one square inch of fabric. Certainly, the best of Chinese embroiderers used threads of floss silk and needles of such fineness, that the eye of one such needle is smaller than a point. Amazing as this may seem, it was not the *raison d'être* of their achievement.

Rather, the uniqueness of Chinese embroidery is to be attributed to the skill of Chinese embroiderers in exploiting one particular type of stitch, namely, the satin stitch, to the limits of its potentialities.

Thus, in depicting a flower, say, a peony, the Chinese embroiderer did not, as would have been expected in normal circumstances, proceed to fill up the spaces within each of the separate petals with closely-laid parallel stitches of one particular colour, in an up-and-down direction, spanning the entire depth of the petal. Instead, she depicted each individual petal as being divided into several narrow strips of spaces arranged one on top of the other, and then proceeded to stitch the spaces within each staggered row with fine coloured silk threads of graduated shadings: the darkest shades were concentrated in the core of the flower, and these became lighter towards the upper edges of the petals.

Depending on the object that was being embroidered, the shadings could be varied to produce imperceptible gradations or more articulated changes of colour. Thus, in fig. 56, the two large pink peony blossoms are depicted in coloured silk threads of fine shadings, graduating from scarlet red to the palest shades of pink, while in fig. 57, the lotus blossom is more dramatically highlighted by various shades of purple, radiating outwards as it were, from the darkest hues to almost pure white.

On the other hand, the red-crested crane (see fig. 56) with its wings outstretched, and standing on one leg as if about to make a graceful leap,

Fig. 56 An embroidered panel executed on red satin, part of a larger panel originally meant to be an ornamental drape for covering one of those square, throne-like blackwood chairs. The main design is dominated by a prancing, red-crested crane (now an endangered species in China) with its magnificent wings stretched out, and blossoms of a tree-peony. The workmanship is of a superior quality, and the satin stitches are extremely fine. Length: 20 inches. Width: 17 inches. Probably of late nineteenth/early twentieth century. Author's collection.

Fig. 57 The two necktie-shaped embroidered hangings were traditionally used to decorate the red-and-gold, four-poster wedding bed. The yellow embroidered panel – reputed to have been a Seah Liang Seah family heirloom – is of excellent workmanship: the motifs have a naturalistic quality and is typical of the best of nineteenth-century Chinese embroidery. The green embroidered panel is said to have come from Penang; its decorative motifs are all executed in the Pekinese stitch and outlined with gold thread couchings. Nineteenth century. Author's collection.

is given a more dramatic portrayal. Note that the two outstretched wings are depicted as consisting of a series of long and prominently large feathers, each of which is executed in oblique satin stitches using two colours only, namely, blue and white. However, the inner edge feather is stitched with shiny threads of a deep cobalt blue, followed by an intermediate strip of lighter blue, and an outer edge of shimmering white. The result is a crane of striking dignity.

The remaining parts of the bird's anatomy are also rendered in satin stitches. But notice, for example, how cunningly the stitches representing the plumage on the neck, the breast and the underbelly are depicted. Instead of using plain, parallel satin stitches, the embroiderer employed long and slanting overlapping stitches to convey a texture of fine feathers. As for the scale-like feathers on the back of the body, small stem stitches of light blue threads were used to outline scale-shaped cells and then filled in with slanting satin stitches. A series of three-pronged, fern stitches provided the finishing touches.

Voiding

Another feature of traditional Chinese embroidery which was widely acknowledged by most European embroiderers as an original contribution of the Chinese, was the art of voiding. As the name implies, voiding refers to a very narrow strip of empty space which separates any two related parts of an embroidered object, such as, for example, the different petals of a flower, or the principal venations of a leaf.

Voiding, as seen in most representative samples of old Chinese embroidery, was intended mainly to serve as outlines for delineating the principal features peculiar to any object, be it a living organism or a man-made artefact. One obvious way of outlining a particular design is to use gold thread couchings to delineate the main features of a satin-stitched pattern. And this technique has indeed been applied in Chinese and nonya embroideries (see fig. 58).

However, outlining with gold threads often results in a *cloisonné* effect which may or may not be to some people's taste. Another method of outlining is to use short and slanted stem stitches of a darker or lighter colour as the case may be, to bring out the detailed features of a particular decorative motif. Stem stitches have been used with great effect to enhance the finer details, but

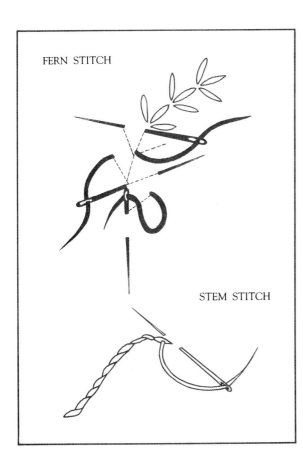

FERN STITCH

STEM STITCH

Fig. 58 Segment of a larger embroidered panel showing the exclusive application of the satin stitch and voiding to delineate the expressive colours and structural details of Penang-styled peony blossoms. Note, in particular, how well the voidings for the petals and the venations of leaves are articulated. This is one of the few examples of Straits Chinese embroidery in which the art of voiding is so clearly expressed. Late nineteenth/early twentieth century. From Penang. Collection of Mrs Ho Wing Meng.

they were rarely used for the main outlines.

Voiding is seen at its best in decorative motifs wholly rendered in satin stitches. It does not come out well with embroidered patterns done in chain stitches, Peking knots or seed knots, because the loops and knots which characterized these stitches, give a relief effect when closely packed together, and are best exploited with gold thread couchings. Hence, voidings were never used in embroidered pieces which were largely executed in either chain stitches or Peking knots.

On the other hand, satin stitches give a flatter and smoother texture which in turn, impart a characteristic sheen to the design. It is also easier to produce subtle shades of colours with satin stitches. Hence, satin-stitched embroidery lends itself more readily to the application of voiding, which is nothing more than a technique of spacing stitches by exposing narrow strips of empty spaces between stitched-up areas.

In this sense, voiding is merely a labour-saving device which enhances the aesthetic quality of a piece of embroidery without, at the same time, involving additional stitchwork. To borrow a popular saying, voiding 'kills two birds with one stone'.

Some very fine pieces of embroidery have been created out of satin stitches alone, and the best of them, reputedly made during the reign of Qianlong (1736–95) in Canton, were said to excel paintings in the variety, gradation of colours and smoothness of texture simulating the more painterly qualities of brushstrokes.

Straits Chinese embroidery is derived from the same tradition of craftsmanship, although the Straits nonyas preferred what was called the

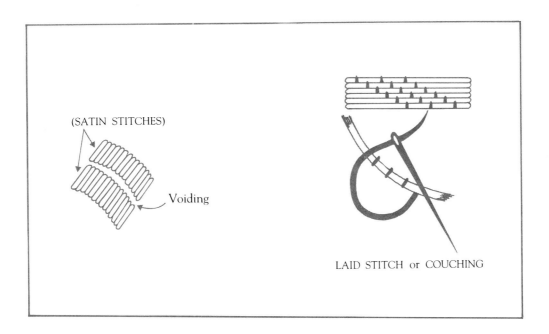

(SATIN STITCHES)

Voiding

LAID STITCH or COUCHING

chi wen (绮紊) or satin stitch tradition of Chinese embroidery to the *duan chan* (缎缠) or seed stitch tradition.

In my opinion, the best of Straits Chinese embroidery executed in satin stitches do not compare with the better ones from China; nor, for that matter, did the nonyas master the art of voiding with the finesse of their counterparts in China. Nonetheless, nonya embroideries possessed a certain freshness and originality. For one thing, they did not slavishly imitate Chinese motifs and designs *ad nauseum*; they merely borrowed the techniques of stitchery and a small selection of traditional motifs to create distinctive types of needlework which are at once Chinese in origin, but Straits Chinese in character and expression.

From what we have said thus far, most of the *larger* pieces of embroidery found in old Straits Chinese homes must, on stylistic grounds alone, be of Chinese origin rather than of local workman-ship. However, they should not, for this reason, be excluded from our descriptions of Straits Chinese embroidery, because needlework of this sort was largely made to Straits Chinese specifications.

In the days gone by, these artefacts were regularly used by well-to-do families to mark important occasions such as weddings, the Chinese New Year, All Souls' Day and birthdays of some elderly patriarch and matriarch; and they included embroidered ornaments, ceremonial costumes, panels, hangings and drapes. These articles became inextricably associated with the cultural heritage of the Straits Chinese simply by being adopted into the customs and traditions of the community.

Among these larger and more conspicuous pieces of embroidery, are long rectangular drapes meant for the bridal chairs and carved blackwood (*Dalbergia*) chairs, ornamental hangings of various sizes for the altar-tables and ancestral tables, drapes for doors and windows, bedspreads, long embroidered panels simulating Chinese scrolled paintings, the ceremonial costumes of the bride and groom, embroidered lanterns, embroidered parasols, table-covers, and so on.

The more knowledgeable elderly babas and nonyas will verify that many of these were imported from China, especially from Canton and Shanghai. I was told that before the War, a number of Chinese embroidery shops in Georgetown, Penang, hired professional China-trained embroiderers to fabricate the larger panels for Straits Chinese homes, Chinese shops and business organizations such as the various *kongsis*.

Whether embroidery shops of this type were found in Malacca and Singapore, has yet to be confirmed. Although there were many shops dealing in Chinese embroideries, it is probable that they were mostly agents-cum-retailers which imported large quantities of ready-made embroidery from Canton, Hong Kong, Swatow, Amoy and Shanghai for retailing to local customers, and for export to other towns throughout Southeast Asia.

Thus, other things being equal, the size of a piece of embroidery is a good indication of its provenance. But more than that, the designs and types of stitches commonly employed, provide further corroborative evidence one way or another. As already indicated before, the motifs of traditional Chinese embroidery designs were more varied, resembling very closely those used on porcelain, gold and silverwork, *cloisonné*, giltwood carvings and paintings. Straits Chinese embroidery motifs, on the other hand, were restricted to the ubiquitous phoenix and peony supplemented occasionally by magpies and butterflies. As for the types of stitchings employed, the Chinese used a large variety of stitches centred on the satin stitch and the Peking stitch. The nonyas, however, preferred the satin stitch and its variations.

There are several explanations why the bigger embroidered panels had to be bought ready-made

either from the local haberdashery or embroidery manufacturers in Canton and Shanghai. Firstly, while only a small minority of traditional nonyas were really gifted in the art of embroidery, the majority were at best passable embroiderers. Since the stitching of a large panel several feet long and wide with complex designs, was a job which required the combined skills and patience of at least two embroiderers working simultaneously, most nonyas were simply unequipped for the task.

Secondly, there is no evidence, as far as I have been able to ascertain, that the former generation of nonyas regularly worked on embroidery frames or *pidangans* larger than, say, 24 inches by 16 inches, though there was no reason why *pidangans* bigger than the standard portable ones could not have been constructed. Big embroidery frames measuring, say, 6 feet by 3 feet were practically non-existent in old Straits Chinese homes; and it was simply impossible to execute the bigger embroidered panels without such frames.

And thirdly, since most traditional nonyas were either housewives or domestic helpers who had to devote a good part of their daily life to various household chores, it was never possible for them to devote more than a few hours at best, to their needlework. Since big embroidered panels required a prodigious amount of time and labour, it was more convenient for the wealthier babas to buy ready-made embroideries made to their specifications, than to have their womenfolk slave endlessly at their *pidangans*.

By about the second or the third decade of this century, it was already possible for the middle-income families to hire various assortments of embroidered articles of adornment and attire required of a traditional Straits Chinese wedding. Special hiring agencies provided these things as well as the services of the traditional *sang-ke-m* and *pak-chindeh* (i.e. the mistress- and master-of-ceremonies) at prices which many more Straits Chinese families could afford.

The advent of such hiring agencies was thus a great boon, especially for those families which preferred to celebrate every wedding according to elaborate ancient rites. They made it unnecessary thereafter, for many a nonya damsel to spend countless hours of tedious work toiling with threads and needles at their embroidery and beadwork.

From the viewpoint of the older generation, the availability of such hiring services meant that they no longer had to worry about spending large sums of money acquiring expensive embroideries from China – and fine Chinese embroideries have always been expensive.[17] But as the Straits Chinese have always been a proud people, the rich continued to buy their embroidered paraphernalia to preserve their upper-class status, while the middle-class preached the virtue of needlecraft as a feminine asset of inestimable value.

Tapestry

Thus far, I have avoided mentioning tapestry in my account of Straits Chinese embroidery for two reasons. Firstly, tapestry which in Chinese is called *ge si* (割丝), or literally, 'cut threads', is not a form of stitching which embroidery is, but a special kind of weaving. A weaver sitting at a loom will manipulate a movable shuttle, and this action will interlace woof threads into the warps to create aesthetic patterns.

In *ge si* weaving, the various coloured woof threads (in Chinese tapestry they are *silk* threads) which go into the creation of the patterns are never woven right across the entire width of the warp threads, but stop short at the borders where the patterns end. If one holds a piece of Chinese silk tapestry with, say, a pattern of peony, against the light, the space occupied by the floral spray looks as if it had been 'cut' out as a separate block from the rest of the fabric – thus the name *ge si*.

Secondly, Chinese tapestries are conspicuously absent from traditional Straits Chinese homes in the Straits Settlements. There are, of course, hand-woven cloths-of-gold known as *kain songket*, and these include *sarungs*, tablecloths, wrappers for the bridal jewellery, etc., made by Malay weavers in Kelantan and Trengganu. No disused weaving looms of any sort have been found in old Straits Chinese homes, and *dewangga*, the Malay word for tapestry, is never used in the baba patois. The Straits Chinese probably regarded weaving as menial work which they studiously avoided.

But Chinese tapestries have always been available not only in China, but also in local embroidery shops. For more than a thousand years Chinese emperors and Court officials have had sumptuous dragon robes and garments specially woven to their specifications. And if the Straits Chinese had wanted to, they could have had all their wedding costumes, drapes, altar-cloths and bed covers, etc., made out of *ge si* tapestries. There is however no evidence that they ever took a fancy to tapestries woven in China. We can only speculate as to why they preferred embroideries to tapestries.

From an aesthetic point of view, tapestry patterns have a tendency to come out somewhat stiffer and more stylized than embroidered patterns with their subtle shadings and other more painterly qualities. This is because the positionings of the various patterns in a tapestry are rigidly determined by the intersections of the warp and woof threads: it is like creating designs within a network of tiny squares.

Besides, while the variations of stitches in embroidery help to simulate the surface textures of living and inanimate objects, creating beautiful patterns, only a weave-like texture typical of all woven fabrics can be produced in tapestries. Thus, the effects produced by tapestries are much less dramatic and spontaneous. No wonder then, that the Straits Chinese ignored Chinese tapestries altogether.

10
Categories of
Straits Chinese Embroidery

W E HAVE NOW described and analyzed in detail the distinctive characteristics distinguishing Straits Chinese embroidery from the more traditional needlework fabricated by embroiderers in China for Chinese communities in Southeast Asia. We have noted in particular, that although Straits Chinese and Chinese embroideries were both derived from the same tradition of needlework insofar as the fabrics, designs and techniques of stitchery are concerned, they do differ significantly. For example, embroidered panels of Penang origin were invariably embellished with fringes of beaded panels often complemented with tassels and spangles. Chinese embroideries may or may not sport decorative fringes, but Rocaille beads are never used.[18]

In the remainder of this section, I propose to select for more detailed treatment several of the three broad categories of Straits Chinese embroidery found in old Straits Chinese homes, including the handiwork of traditional Malay embroiderers for purposes of clarification and comparison.

The three main types of embroidery to be considered here are (1) small rectangular embroidered panels, with or without fringes of narrow, threaded bead-panels sporting short tassels, traditionally used as table-covers, panels for picture-frames, ornamental hangings, pillow and bolster cases; (2) embroidered articles of Malay or Indonesian origin, namely, *selendang*, *sapu tangan*, *kasut*

manek, *kepala bantal* and *sarung kebaya*; and (3) those larger panels, hangings and drapes for altar-tables, lintels of doors and windows and the wedding bed. Under this category must also be included ceremonial costumes for the bride and groom and their accessories.

SMALL PANELLED EMBROIDERIES

As indicated previously, one reason why Straits Chinese embroidery tends to be confined to needlework of smaller dimensions, was that the traditional nonyas always worked on slate or rectangular embroidery frames no bigger than 24 inches by 14 inches. Besides, a nonya embroiderer always worked alone on a piece of embroidered panel, never in collaboration with one or two others.

However, in embroidery factories in Soochow, Shanghai or Canton, it was quite common for two or more embroiderers to collaborate at stitching a large embroidered panel, because two pairs of nimble hands are obviously faster than one. Perhaps, for this reason, the smaller nonya embroideries tend to display a more personal and distinctive style of workmanship, whereas large embroideries executed by several embroiderers, each specializing in some aspects of the ornamental

Fig. 59 This petite rectangular embroidered silk panel with five beaded tassels on both ends, is probably the most beautiful example of Straits Chinese embroidery that I have seen in many years. The design is dominated by two large peony blossoms (they look more like dahlias to me) executed with superb skill in satin stitches. A prominent border running all round the panel is filled with rose-like peonies. The sheer freshness of the colours and the sheen on the silk threads, give the impression that this embroidered panel was only fabricated yesterday. Collection of Mrs Grace Saw.

designs, the colour scheme preferred and the quality of the workmanship, is different. It is like listening to the same piece of classical musical composition played either on the violin or the piano by different musicians. One may hear the same composition several times without being overcome by sheer boredom, because each interpretation is a new experience. For this reason, it is not unusual for students of Straits Chinese embroidery to collect several pieces of the same type of embroidered panels and still find pleasure in contemplating them, since no two pieces are ever identical.

Some of the most distinctive examples of such embroidered table-covers or pillow-covers (and the bigger of these oblong panels can be used interchangeably) sporting rose-like peonies in maroon red were made by the Penang nonyas, and the workmanship, invariably done in satin stitches, rival some of the best from Canton (see fig. 59), not only in the neatness and fineness of the stitchery, but also for their attractive colours and pleasing designs.

The Penang nonyas, more than their counterparts in Singapore and Malacca, made it a rule to attach two narrow strips of glittering beadwork with short tassels to the widths of their small oblong embroidered panels, apparently to give an added touch of luxury to these already showy

design, tend to be more nondescript from a stylistic point of view.

If you compare, say, two rectangular table-covers meant for one of those blackwood side-tables flanked by two chairs, done by two different nonya embroiderers, you will notice at once that while the two panels are of identical dimensions, everything else about them including the choice of

Fig. 62 This pair of ornamental hangings for the wedding bed from the heirloom of a peranakan Chinese family in Indonesia, is somewhat unusual. Its main decorative motifs consist of figures of the eight Taoist immortals and a pair of *qilins*. Sequins and beaded tassels give an added glamour to these embroidered panels.
Collection of Donald Harper.

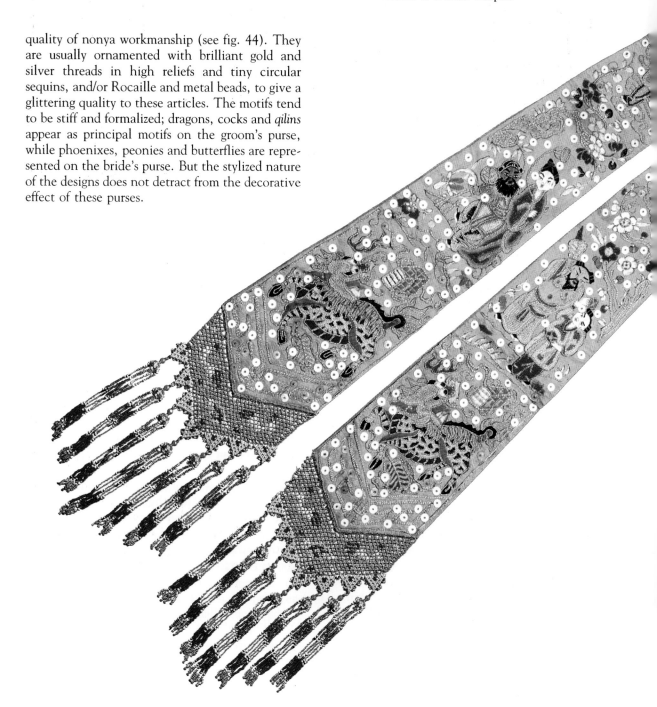

quality of nonya workmanship (see fig. 44). They are usually ornamented with brilliant gold and silver threads in high reliefs and tiny circular sequins, and/or Rocaille and metal beads, to give a glittering quality to these articles. The motifs tend to be stiff and formalized; dragons, cocks and *qilins* appear as principal motifs on the groom's purse, while phoenixes, peonies and butterflies are represented on the bride's purse. But the stylized nature of the designs does not detract from the decorative effect of these purses.

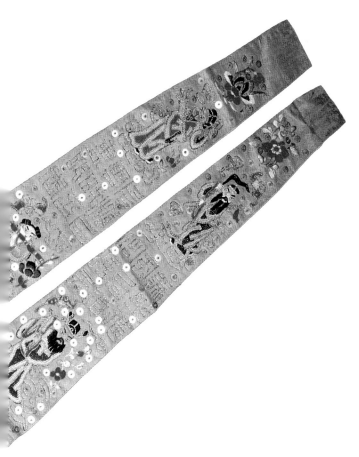

Oval cap

Another item of interest in this category of small, pretty embroidered objects, is the flat-topped, oval cap worn by the groom's attendant. One such example in Mrs Ho Wing Meng's collection, is made out of crimson red velvet with several layers of paper and cotton fabric backings pasted to the underside to provide the necessary stiffening. It consists of three separate embroidered panels, namely, a pointed oval panel and two crescent-shaped panels sewn together along the edges. The embroidered motifs, consisting chiefly of delicate floral and foliated motifs, with birds, butterflies and other insects, are usually executed in fine satin stitches. Sequins are frequently added to give an extra glitter to the already ornate and colourful designs. Occasionally the caps are ornamented with small Rocaille beads.

Gewgaws

Ornamental hangings for the wedding bed, the so-called 'gewgaws' (see fig. 36), are among the more irresistibly attractive embroideries of nonya workmanship. Such articles are made in the round, with the obverse and reverse sides sporting the same embroidered motifs. Each set of 'gewgaws' consists of three solid panels connected by beaded tassels and decorative bobs wrapped with a network of dangling silk threads.

The fabrication of each of these ornamental articles which usually depict a mandarin duck, butterflies, peony blossoms and other appropriate wedding symbols, requires a considerable amount of work.

Firstly, the design has to be traced on two separate pieces of silk such that one silk panel carries its obverse side of the design, while the other silk panel bears the same design traced in reverse order. Next, the two panels are mounted on an embroidery frame and the stitching commences. Fine coloured silk threads are used for executing satin stitches on the design.

Very often, the general outlines of the different parts of the design are delineated with gold thread couchings to highlight the more significant features. As soon as the stitchings are completed, the two embroidered panels are removed from the embroidery frames and then strengthened with several layers of thin cotton backings pasted to their undersides. The panels are then left to dry for several days.

Next the outer edges of the two embroidered panels are cut away with the help of a pair of sharp pointed scissors. Care must be taken to ensure that the embroidered threads are not accidentally snipped off. This done, the two separate panels are laid front to back to ensure that all their outer edges are identically matched, before they are sewn together at the outer seams. The embroiderer sews along the edges but leaves a gap into which cotton wool is tightly stuffed, until the two panels begin to swell somewhat to give a three-dimensional solidity to the article. Finally, the seams in the gap are stitched together.

Fig. 63 A pair of circular ornaments executed in cut- or pierced work and embroidered on both the obverse and reverse sides. The theme of these decorative ornaments is interesting as it is unusual: it shows a flowering spray of star fruits. The star fruit, a tropical plant, does not occur in the traditional Chinese repertoire of auspicious symbols. Apart from this unusual feature, the execution of the voidings in this cut-work requires steady hands and concentration: the puncher which cuts out the voidings must be handled carefully so that it does not accidentally cut through the embroidered designs. Diameter: 6¼ inches. Late nineteenth/early twentieth century. From Penang. Collection of Mrs Ho Wing Meng.

Cut-work ornaments

Another type of distinctive Straits Chinese embroidery is the circular cut-work ornament, about seven-and-a-half inches in diameter on the average, which is stiffened with several layers of paper-cum-cotton fabrics. An unusual pair of such circular ornaments executed in cut-work (see fig. 63) is embroidered on both the obverse and reverse sides. Gold threads were used for outlining and for securing the seams together. Circular ornaments of this type were meant to be hung either on the wall or attached to ceremonial furniture in the bridal chamber. These came mostly from Penang.

Fig. 64 Three circular embroidered ornaments mounted on 10 to 12 layers of paper and cotton backings and executed in cut-work. These three ornaments differ from the ones in Fig. 63 in that the embroidered motifs occur on only one side. The bottom is simply pasted over with a piece of scarlet cotton cloth. Such ornaments could either be laid flat on a table, or hung from a wall. Widths vary from 5¾ inches to 8 inches. Late nineteenth/early twentieth century. From Penang. Collection of Mrs Ho Wing Meng.

The technique employed here is practically the same as that used for making those 'gewgaws', except that these cut-work ornaments were embroidered on one side only – the cotton or paper backings being intended merely to provide a rigid support for needlework (see fig. 64). Some were embroidered on plain white cotton fabric while others were done on silk.

By and large, the main design outlines are delineated with gold thread couchings, sometimes with double gold threads. Unlike embroidered panels meant for the 'gewgaws', the void spaces separating the various features of the design have to be cut away. Since some of these ornaments are up to a few millimetres thick, the cut-work must be executed with utmost care to ensure that the knife or puncher does not accidentally slice through the edges of the embroidered stitches. Cut-work ornaments of this type are peculiar to Straits Chinese embroidery from Penang. They are found nowhere else in this region – certainly not among the varieties of embroidered articles made in China.

Fig. 65 A *sapu tangan* (Malay word for handkerchief) is an ornamental, embroidered panel of quatrefoil shape with two elongated sides joined together. Embroidered entirely with gold threads and sequins against a dark green velvet backing, this *sapu tangan* has tassels of fine, red silk. Late nineteenth century. From Malacca. Collection of Mrs Ho Wing Meng.

ITEMS OF MALAY OR INDONESIAN ORIGIN

Since the Straits Chinese are the descendants of immigrant Chinese, Malay and also Indian racial stocks, their traditional culture was, in some significant respects, influenced by old Malay and Hindu-Malay customs and traditions. It comes as no surprise, therefore, that some of their embroidery items (and beadwork) should bear close resemblance with corresponding articles found in Malay customs and practices.

Thus, articles such as the *selendang*, the *sapu tangan*, the *kasut manek*, the *bantal* plates and the *sarung kebaya*, hinted strongly of Malay origin, since the Straits Chinese adopted the Malay names originally used to denote these artefacts. Besides, there are no equivalents of such embroidered articles among the entire repertoire of traditional Chinese needlework.

Selendang

The *selendang* is a shawl worn over the shoulder (either right or left) by the older generation of nonyas. Among the beebiks, as the older nonyas are referred to, it was customary for them to wear the *baju panjang* which is really an older version of the *sarung kebaya*, in the sense that the *baju* was an elongated *kebaya* reaching down to the knee. With the older beebiks, the *selendang* was an essential component of the *baju panjang*.

Actually, it is a large square piece of fabric (usually of flowered cotton, batik or silk) more than twice the standard size of a man's handkerchief, and it is always folded twice over to form a triangular piece – thus the Hokkien name 'Sah Kok Pau', literally, a three-cornered folding. One of the two longer ends of this triangular 'handkerchief' is secured to the topmost *kerosang* (or jewelled brooch) and the rest of the *selendang* is draped over the shoulder. It served as a kind of hand-towel-cum-napkin.

Sometimes the *selendang* is designed in the shape of a long rectangular panel (usually of embroidered silk) about 24 inches long and 3½ – 4 inches wide. The space inside the panel is usually stitched with motifs of flowers, birds, butterflies and other auspicious symbols connected with marriage.

In Mr Peter Wee's collection, there is a bridal *selendang* of this description. Another equally distinctive piece, reputedly said to have come from the Seah Liang Seah family, is more triangular in shape and ornamented with embroidered motifs of phoenixes, peonies, lotuses and butterflies on a background of bright yellow silk (see fig. 52). *Selendangs* of this type were used by the bride on the third and twelfth day of the wedding ceremonies, when she visited her father- and mother-in-law's home to pay her respects.

The bridal *selendang* was never used as a handkerchief or a napkin: its function was purely ornamental and ceremonial. Nor, for that matter, was it ever used as a head-scarf, as with the

Fig. 66 Straits Chinese wedding slippers. The three larger pairs shown on the right were intended for the groom, while the two smaller pairs were meant for the bride. Until the early decades of the present century, every potential bride had to learn how to embroider her own slippers as well as those of her husband-to-be, and the fine and intricate workmanship of these jewel-like slippers clearly testify to the skill and artistry of nonyas of a bygone generation. From Penang.

selendang used by Malay women. This is because the Straits nonya always wore her hair-knot or bun, known as *sanggal siput*, high on the back of her head. She also inserted three large silvergilt hairpins into her hair-knot. A *selendang* tied over her head would immediately disrupt the orderly positioning of the hairpins and impose an intolerable strain upon her hair-bun.

Sapu tangan

The *sapu tangan* has already been referred to in the previous section on beadwork (see fig. 65). Embroidered versions of *sapu tangan* are also available in private collections in Singapore and Malaysia. The *sapu tangan* looks like a pentagon panel with two elongated sides meeting at a point; and in the days gone by, it was always worn by the bride

as a complementary ornament to the *sarung kebaya* and the *selendang* on the third day of a typical Straits Chinese wedding. The *sapu tangan* always came with a little metal ring attached to the apex end, and this little ring was slipped into the fourth finger of the left hand, thus allowing the broad end of the *sapu tangan* to dangle forward.

Kasut manek/sulam – embroidered variety

The *kasut manek*, or beaded slippers, have already been described in Part I, except that in baba patois, the term *kasut manek* is loosely used to include slippers which have been embroidered with silk threads, gold and silver threads, sequins and even appliquéd silver ornaments (see fig. 66). Generally, embroidered slippers have their decorative motifs raised in high reliefs.

Fig. 67 Two pairs of rare but authentic wedding shoes embroidered exclusively in gold threads against a scarlet background. Such ceremonial wedding shoes were worn by traditional Straits Chinese brides and grooms on the wedding day, when they put on their voluminous and ornately embroidered silk costumes and jewelled head-dresses. These shoes must not be confused with the commoner wedding slippers, many of which can still be seen in old Straits Chinese homes. The smaller pair of beaded shoes at the bottom was probably intended for one of the two bridal attendants. Properties of Mrs Ho Wing Meng and Mr Peter Wee.

The method of embroidering nonya and baba slippers (the difference, incidentally, is merely that of size, with the male's slippers having a larger sole) was the same as that used for other types of nonya embroidery; except that in the case of slippers and other related articles, velvets were preferred to silk or cotton.

For relief effects, the nonyas cut out thin strips of cardboard about 1 mm thick and pasted them on to those parts of the outlines which were intended to be highlighted. The designs are then embroidered with silk threads and gold and silver threads by applying the long and short stitch, the alternat-ing stitch, the overlapping stitch and couched and laid work.

Gold and silver threads, being thicker, were usually made for higher relief work (see fig. 67). But coloured silk threads when embroidered in satin stitches gave a smoother texture and charac-teristic sheen unattainable by gold and silver threads. Some of the extant examples of old *kasut manek* are entirely embroidered with gold and silver threads, tinsels and metal sequins, while others of more conservative designs are embroi-dered with coloured silk threads.

The fabrication of *kasut sulam* of this type

Fig. 68 Three pairs of embroidered nonya slippers executed almost entirely with silver threads, silver wires and sequins. These slippers differ from the ones used by the bride during her wedding in that these have heels. Collection of Mr Peter Wee.

probably became a lost art some time during the late twenties or thereabouts, as extant samples of such slippers are usually estimated by most babas and nonyas, as well as antique dealers, with whom I discussed the question of dating, to be at least sixty or seventy years old.

Whereas *kasut manek* are still being made by some old *tukang kasut* (shoemaker) and perhaps a handful of old nonyas in Singapore, Malacca and Penang, practically all extant pieces of *kasut sulam* that I have seen in old baba homes and in private collections are, without doubt, of vintage workmanship. So, while it is still possible to hunt out some old nonyas who would be willing to stitch a pair of beaded toe-covers for *kasut manek*, it is practically impossible to find anyone who will undertake to embroider a pair of wedding slippers with intricate relief patterns and appliquéd work after the manner of old *kasut sulam*.

Fig. 69 The most remarkable thing about these three *bantal* plates with silk embroidered designs is in the exclusive use of geometric patterns. My first impression was that they were of East European (Rumanian, Bulgarian, Yugoslavian or Hungarian) origins. But Mr Harper assured me that he procured these articles from an old peranakan home in Java (or was it Sumatra?) and he was categorically informed that they were the handiwork of some old nonyas. It then occurred to me that the designs were inspired by aborigine designs from Sumba Island or those of other tribes in Sumatra. Dimension of the largest panel: 6 inches by 3½ inches. Collection of Donald Harper.

Bantal plates

Embroidered *bantal* plates (i.e. pillow and bolster panels) are relatively few and far between. Some *bantal* plates of unusual designs from Indonesia have already been alluded in Chapter 7. But *bantal* panels sporting designs in which small Rocaille beads have been stitched against velvet backings of deep maroon, dark blue and dark green, used to be seen in antique shops in Malacca some fifteen to twenty years ago. They appear to have been very popular with Malacca chettiars (i.e. Tamils who

Fig. 70 An example of the finer of Indonesian *kebaya* with ornate floral lacework decorating the lower half of the front, the sleeves and the neckline. The white cotton fabric is of Swiss voile, regarded by the nonyas as the most suitable material for making *kebayas*. The ornamental, floral lacework is done by machine, but the cut-work and voidings requiring pulled and drawn threads, have to be executed manually. And when the ornamental lacework is as extensive as in this *kebaya*, the workmanship is time-consuming and demands a high degree of manual dexterity. Notice that the frontal hems of Indonesian *kebayas* are longer than those of Straits Chinese origins. Collection of Donald Harper.

had adopted Straits Chinese culture or who married into Straits Chinese families), and then with the babas themselves. However, most extant pieces of *bantal* plates are in silver; and as I have stated elsewhere[20] silver *bantal* plates were the most common type of silver articles found in old Straits Chinese homes. Incidentally, the traditional mainland Chinese did not attach *bantal* plates to their bridal pillows and bolsters.

Kebaya

The traditional *kebaya* is a kind of long-sleeved, body-hugging outer garment reaching below the waist and open in front (see fig. 70). The frontal hems are secured together not by buttons, but by a set of three leaf-shaped *kerosangs*, or jewelled brooches executed in open or pierced work, and connected together by short chains.

Fig. 71 Samples of batik *sarungs* traditionally used by Straits nonyas. Unlike Javanese women who generally preferred sombre coloured batiks with shades of brown and black, Straits nonyas regularly patronised the ornate and brightly coloured *sarungs* made in Pekalongan in Java. *Sarungs* with predominantly blue designs were used only during mourning. Collection of Mrs Josephine Wee.

For their *kebayas*, the nonyas preferred voile, the French or Swiss variety of fine cotton fabric. Voile comes in a variety of colours, such as white, slate blue, violet blue, cherry red, lemon yellow, saffron yellow, apple green, pink and *café au lait* brown (see fig. 71). The *kebaya* is always worn to complement the traditional batik *sarung*.

This is not the place to discourse in any detail the art of batik design or the different kinds of batik *sarung* found in Indonesia and Malaysia, because the batik *sarung* is a special kind of painted or printed fabric and is thus not related to needlework of any kind. I merely wish to mention in passing that the Straits nonyas have always preferred the Pekalongan type of batik *sarungs* to most other types of Javanese *sarungs*, with the exception of *kain songket* (cloth-of-gold) *sarungs* from Kelantan. This is because the Pekalongan batiks always came with dense and flamboyant designs of huge floral blossoms, peacocks, birds,

ducks and butterflies, all vividly dyed in bright reds, greens, blues, yellows, purples and browns. Compared with the highly formalized designs dyed in sombre browns and blacks of East Javanese batiks from Jogjakarta and Surakarta, the Pekalongan batiks are a riot of the brightest hues; and, of course, the nonyas loved their ornate exuberance.

The *kebaya* as we know it today, is a garment of fairly recent origin (see fig. 72). It is believed to have made its appearance in Indonesia, particularly, Medan (in Sumatra) and Batavia (now Jakarta, in Java) about the time of the First World War. But by the early twenties, it was widely accepted as the standard costume of all the younger generation of nonyas in the Straits Settlements. Until then (if old photographs of nonyas taken before 1910 or thereabouts are anything to go by) it was customary for all nonyas, both young and old, to wear the knee-length *baju panjang* in complement with the batik *sarung*.

Fig. 72 This light pink *kebaya* belonging to Mrs Josephine Wee, is ornamented with purple and yellow flowers. Notice that the frontal hems of local nonyas are shorter than those of Indonesian *kebayas*.

Fig. 73 Details of the lacework (*sulam*) on a Swiss voile *kebaya* in rich imperial purple. The formalized white floral motifs and pale green leaves set against a fine network of red and purple greatly enliven this *kebaya*. Collection of Mrs Josephine Wee.

As far as the embroidered designs on *kebayas* are concerned, the standard practice was to confine the ornamental works to a narrow border of between half-an-inch to one-and-a-quarter inches along the entire length of the outer hems of the garment, including the fringes of the sleeves. In more elaborately embroidered *kebayas*, the designs on the frontal hems fan outwards and downwards from waist level, until they cover entire lower portions of the *kebaya*. As for the back portion, the designs spread upwards to form a triangular pattern. Sometimes, polka dots or picots are added to cover the unembroidered portions of the *kebaya* (see fig. 73).

Since the voice used in *kebayas* is a delicate fabric of fine network texture, Indonesian embroiderers decided that the techniques of stitchery most suitable for decorating the hems, the lower frontal portions, the back and the sleeves, until the advent of machine embroidery, was a combination of cut-work, drawn thread, satin stitch and buttonhole stitch. The idea was to create lacework designs which would harmonize with the web-like texture of voile. To this end, they had to employ either the satin stitch or the buttonhole stitch to outline the main motifs – like flowers and fruits.

The chief advantage of using either the satin stitch or the buttonhole stitch is that they prevent the edges from fraying when the void spaces connecting the different motifs are cut away to create a lacework effect. The satin and buttonhole

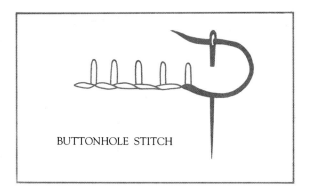

BUTTONHOLE STITCH

stitches are also useful for securing the bars, that is, the warp or woof threads left behind after some of the threads in the fabric have been drawn out. But the labour required for embroidering lacework

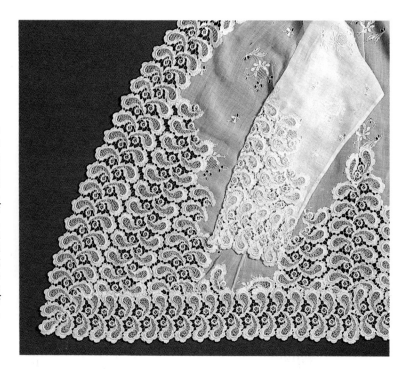

Fig. 74 White *kebaya* with elegant floral lacework executed in white silk threads. In traditional Straits Chinese and peranakan Chinese customs, white was the colour of mourning; so this *kebaya*, obviously intended for a well-to-do nonya, was used only during the mourning period. Nonetheless, this *kebaya* is of fine workmanship. Collection of Donald Harper.

Fig. 75 Among the traditional Straits nonyas, the beauty, and correspondingly, the value of a *kebaya* was related to the quality of the embroidered lacework and the extent and intricacy of the designs. Wealthy nonyas prided themselves with *kebayas* of very ornate and fine lacework. This *kebaya*, also belonging to Mrs Josephine Wee, is an example of ornate and fine ornamental designs.

patterns or voile fabrics was slow and painstaking, especially when a lot of cut-work has to be executed. For this reason, the intricate *sulam* work (*sulam* is Malay for 'embroidery') for an expensive *kebaya* required several weeks of slow and steady work.

With the introduction of the sewing machine which could be adapted to execute embroidery stitches of various types, after the Second World War, the task of embroidering *kebayas* with lacework patterns was speeded up considerably. By employing three simple stitches, namely the straight stitch, the satin stitch and the zig-zag stitch, the sewing machine could accomplish much more quickly all the stitching work needed, except cut-work, and drawn- and pulled-thread which still

required manual dexterity of a high order. The embroidered designs found on *kebayas* worn by nonyas nowadays are, almost without exception, stitched by sewing machine. Only the voidings are cut by hand. Still, some people maintain that stitched work by hand is superior in finish and texture (see fig. 74).

Usually, the embroidered patterns in a *kebaya* are all executed in silk threads of one colour only; the colour could be of a lighter or a darker shade than that of the background voile fabric. *Sulam* work done in this manner is most harmonious and pleasing to the eye, no matter how complicated the lacework patterns may be (see fig. 75). Sometimes, however, threads of several colours are employed to highlight different motifs.

A comparison of Straits Chinese and Malay embroidery

I have already dwelt at some length on the differences and similarities between traditional Chinese embroideries and those of Straits Chinese workmanship. I have also highlighted some distinctive features of those items of Straits Chinese embroidery of Malay and Indonesian origin, not only in the superficial sense that their designs were inspired by native archetypes, but also in the fact that the ceremonial functions can be traced to the influence of Malay and Indonesian cultures. However, the effects produced by centuries of cultural assimilation with the natives, while significant to some extent, did not result in the wholesale transformation of their way of living, but only superficial changes in forms and styles – at least as far as the forms and functions of these embroidered artefacts are concerned. The Straits Chinese culture remained largely Chinese in spirit and substance.

The fact that such items of embroidery (and of beadwork in some instances) including *sapu tangan*, *selendang* panels, *kasut manek* and *kasut sulam* (both beaded and embroidered), *kepala bantal* for pillow and bolsters, and the *kebaya*, were given Malay names rather than their Hokkien equivalents in Baba Malay, was a tacit acknowledgement of indebtedness to Malay and Indonesian cultures.

The proof of it is that these articles did not feature in the wedding practices of the more conservative Chinese communities in Southeast Asia and China. However, careful examination will show that the designs on all Straits Chinese embroideries (and beadwork as well) are, without exception, directly borrowed from ancient Chinese art and religious motifs. So, too, are the techniques of stitchery employed. But of that, more presently.

As noted previously, the symbols and art motifs employed in both Straits Chinese and traditional Chinese embroidery, were never chosen simply because they looked beautiful, but rather, because the symbols were traditionally regarded as auspicious (see figs. 49, 52, 57 & 76). Hence, the symbolic motifs appearing on artefacts intended for, say, wedding ceremonies, differ somewhat from those meant for birthday ceremonies or religious offerings. In order to tell the differences between artefacts used for the various types of ceremonies, one must, however, be sufficiently informed concerning the traditional meanings attached to the various symbols commonly used.

Another characteristic of Chinese art motifs, whether they occur in porcelain, paintings, jade and soapstone carvings, wood-carvings, gold and silverwork, tapestry or embroidery, is the marvellous sense of realism and spontaneity with which they are depicted via the different mediums of expression. This is particularly true of flowers and foliage, birds and insects, for which the Chinese have been justly praised in the West.

In Malay embroidery, however, the design was strictly restricted to floral and foliated motifs and/or abstract geometric patterns (see fig. 77). Representations of human and animal figures were, of course, forbidden by the teachings of Islam. But even where floral and foliated designs are concerned, they were never allowed to be realistic portrayals of living flowers. For this reason, there are no graphic representations in Malay embroidery (and weavings as well) of, say, the commonest scented blossoms used by Malay women, such as *bunga meloh* (jasmine), *bunga mawar* (rose), *bunga chempaka* (both the saffron and white varieties), *bunga tongkeng*, *bunga tanjong* and *bunga scudangan*. Malay artists scrupulously stylized their floral and foliated motifs so that the arabesque designs which emerged resembled no living species in nature.

Nor can you expect to find, in Malay needlework, the application of a wide variety of stitches traditionally used by embroiderers elsewhere.

Fig. 76 This long embroidered panel, almost six feet in length, and probably intended for adorning the wedding bed, is embellished with peony blossoms and a pair of phoenixes, butterflies (symbols of conjugal bliss), stags and cranes (symbols of long life). The principal stitch used is the Pekinese knot. Early twentieth century. Collection of Mrs Grace Saw.

Generally, the Malay embroiderers of old needlework did not employ the more popular stitches used in Europe and Asia, namely, the satin stitch, the alternating stitch, the chain stitch, the French knot, the split stitch, the stem stitch, the Pekinese stitch. Malay embroiderers seemed to prefer the couching technique to other types of stitches, as it was extensively used in their needlework.

Malay embroiderers also employed a lot of tinsel materials, especially gold and silver threads of different thicknesses, shapes and textures, for filling all their ornamental designs. Gold and silver threads are usually couched against either a bright satin or a velvet of deep maroon, green or blue. Sequins and tassels with spangles are liberally used on the borders and fringes of embroidered panels, so that they shine with the tremulous lights of metallic tinsels on a Christmas tree. Straits Chinese embroideries look comparatively sombre and archaic.

Fig. 77 Another long embroidered six-feet long panel, this is a bed-runner or mattress panel of old Malay workmanship. The design, of formalized floral patterns executed in high relief work, is unusual in that the main outlines and the more conspicuous features of the floral patterns, are wrapped with thin gold strips and then couched down by thinner gold threads. Golden sequins are liberally sewn against the background of red velvet. While the precept of Islam prohibiting idolatry of any kind dictated the choice of motifs used, there is no doubt that Islamic designs were meant to be aesthetic rather than symbolic. Late nineteenth century. From Malacca. Author's collection.

LARGE PANELLED EMBROIDERIES

The larger pieces of extant embroidery can be divided into two sub-categories: (1) square or rectangular panels, and (2) embroidered costumes.

Of the larger pieces of embroidery found in old Straits Chinese homes, these include drapes for the traditional wedding bed, doors, windows, altar tables, bridal chairs, bed-covers, panels for lintels, and ceremonial wedding costumes made for the bride and groom.

As already noted before, such embroidered panels were all fabricated by professional embroiderers in China to suit the special requirements of different clients in Southeast Asia; very few of the large embroidered panels found in old Straits Chinese homes were fabricated by the nonyas themselves. Nonetheless, during the latter part of the nineteenth century, the more well-to-do Straits Chinese families in the Straits Settlements bought large quantities of Chinese embroidered panels, hangings and costumes made to their specifications to commemorate one or other of their many lavish festivals.

The great bulk of these nineteenth-century embroideries have perished long ago, through neglect, natural wear and tear and, of course, the depredations of World War II. The remnants that somehow managed to survive the vicissitudes of the times, are already in various stages of decay.

Tropical heat and humidity is so unfavourable to the preservation of all natural fabrics, that it is rare indeed to find an old piece of silk embroidery which can be authentically dated to 1870 or 1880 – at least I have not been able to do so. Besides, most examples of antique silk embroideries are undated anyway; and while we know on circumstantial evidence that no extant pieces of embroidery in Straits Chinese homes can be dated before 1800, we have no direct method of ascertaining the age of any particular embroidery as such.

Generally, embroideries of larger dimensions made to Straits Chinese specifications are largely ornamented with floral and foliated motifs (the tree peony and lotus being preferred) usually complemented with phoenixes, several types of birds including magpies, quails, mandarin ducks, storks and cranes, and insects such as butterflies, dragonflies and grasshoppers (see figs. 49 & 76). These differ from embroideries of nonya workmanship in employing a much wider variety of flowers, birds and insects. Occasionally, figures of regally clad officials and court ladies appear in some of the embroidered panels.

However, there is one principal motif in Chinese art which is rarely seen in embroideries made for the Straits Chinese, and that is the dragon. Whereas the dragon is frequently represented in all the splendour befitting this imperial emblem in embroidered panels and hangings made for the more conservative Chinese communities in Southeast Asia, it seldom features in Straits Chinese embroidery. It does not even appear on the wedding costume worn by the bridegroom, even though the dragon is a male symbol.

There are no flying dragons, writhing dragons or rampaging dragons breathing fire and smoke in pursuit of the heavenly pearl, to be seen on those large and showy pieces of needlework which the Straits Chinese proudly display on important occasions. Instead, it is the ubiquitous phoenix, or rather a pair of phoenixes, and after it, in order of precedence, the tree peony (always depicted with attractive blossoms) which takes pride of place in Straits Chinese embroidery. Likewise, figures of Taoist immortals and lohans, court scenes or scenes depicting episodes taken from well-known Chinese operas and literary classics, are largely absent.

The principal background colours of these embroidered panels (see fig. 78) were red (ranging from pink to deep maroon) and green (from the palest shades to apple green). And the ceremonial costumes, drapes and other types of panels used for the wedding ceremonies (and even birthdays and the Chinese New Year) appeared in these two

principal colours. Blue and violet backgrounds
were, however, rarely seen except in embroidered
panels used for draping the catafalque and hearse at
funerals. Blue, and variations of it in darker tones,
was, and still is, the funeral colour for the Chinese
and Straits Chinese alike.

As for the designs which appear on the larger
embroidered pieces, especially when flowers,
foliage, birds, animals and insects are represented,
they are, as usual, rendered with a surprising
degree of realism and spontaneity. Even though
the motifs are now drawn on a bigger scale, thus
requiring larger and more complex stitches for the
fillings and to articulate the surface textures of the
various objects, the final result is still vividly
expressive and naturalistic. Here is another feature
characteristic of Chinese embroidery, namely, that
the design rarely comes across as stiff and lifeless
(see fig. 79).

The principal stitches employed in the bigger
embroidered panels are the same as those used for
the smaller pieces, namely, the satin stitch,
couching, the Pekinese stitch and the seed stitch.
Roughly, they are divided into two broad categories, the *chi wen* (satin stitch) and the *duan chan*

Fig. 78 Long embroidered rectangular panel intended either for the 'front' of the traditional four-poster wedding bed, or perhaps, the lintel of the door leading to the bridal chamber in Penang. One significant feature about old Straits Chinese homes in Penang is the exceptional width and height of their doors. They were definitely taller and wider than the doors of those traditional shop-like houses in Heeren Street (now known as Jalan Tun Tan Cheng Lok) in Malacca. Notice that all the decorative designs on this panel were embroidered in gold threads. Probably of South China provenance. Early twentieth century. Collection of Mrs Grace Saw.

Fig. 79 This impressive altar hanging over 6 feet long and 3½ feet wide, was acquired about eighteen years ago, and is reputedly said to have been an heirloom of the Seah Liang Seah family. The decorative designs on the lower panel were executed largely in gold threads (the colours have not faded) and coloured silk threads, and they are symbolic of a traditional Chinese wedding: huge peony blossoms, a pair of phoenixes, a pair of quails and white birds. The narrow upper panel shows a scene of courtly figures in a garden setting. All the motifs here are exclusively executed in scintillating gold threads. Probably of South China provenance. Late nineteenth century. Author's collection.

Fig. 80 This close-up view of a large embroidered panel, which belonged to an old Penang family, shows details of a phoenix (one of a pair) and peony blossoms on the broad central panel. The floral motifs are all executed with the Pekinese stitch, while the phoenix and the foliage are done in satin stitches. Below the main embroidered panel is a broad fringe of beadwork executed by threading with tassels of coloured silk threads. The embroidered panel is probably of South China provenance, while the beaded panel is of local, nonya workmanship. Collection of Mrs Grace Saw.

(the seed stitch). These stitches are used in complement with gold thread couchings for the larger fillings.

But for the details, the Chinese embroiderer used a larger variety of stitches, including long and short stitches, alternating stitches, overlapping stitches, stem stitches, split stitches, cross stitches,

seed knots, laced stitches, chain stitches and *petit point*.

On the whole, the evidence shows that embroiderers in China were more adept at applying a greater variety of stitches to create special effects of one sort or another, than their nonya counterparts in the Straits Settlements. However, it must

Fig. 81 This lovely rectangular embroidered silk panel, one of a pair, has a light creamy background, and the decorative designs consisting of peonies, deer, antique vases, etc., are executed in fine satin stitches – using pale colours of white, cream, orange, red, blue and green. An exceptional piece of embroidery of Penang workmanship. Length: 16 inches. Width: 8 inches. Collection of Mrs Grace Saw.

not be forgotten that large embroideries were the products of several embroiderers, with each embroiderer executing only one type of stitch.

In nonya embroideries, on the other hand, *one* person had to execute *all* the work from beginning to end, and these included tracing out the patterns on the prescribed piece of silk, stretching out the fabric on the *pidangan*, and finally, the laborious process of filling up all the details with stitches of several sorts. Since a piece of nonya embroidery was always done by one person, the skill required was probably greater and more demanding than that required of a professional embroiderer who specialized at executing only one type of stitch. Nonya embroidery is, after all, no less respectable than Chinese embroidery (see figs. 80 & 81).

Square or rectangular panels

The largest and most impressive pieces are drapes for the wedding bed, bed-covers, door curtains and altar hangings. Drapes specially made for the Straits Chinese wedding bed are rarely encountered. During the past fifteen years or so, I have seen no more than five complete sets of drapes for wedding beds in a fine state of preservation.

A complete set of bed-curtains comes in four principal pieces measuring a total length of twenty-two feet and a width or height of five feet. Those intended for brass beds are higher – about eight feet. The frontal drape is usually divided into two equal rectangular panels, three feet wide and five feet high: this is to enable the frontal drapes to be parted more conveniently and secured to each of the two frontal posts of the wedding bed.

The principal background colours of these drapes are lime green or scarlet red, and the more expensive ones have designs embroidered on damask silks. The decorative designs, usually of phoenixes, storks, mandarin ducks, peonies or sprigs of flowers scattered all over the fabric, are usually executed in fine gold thread couchings, or else, a combination of satin stitches of silk threads and gold thread couchings.

One set of bed-curtains which was shown to me in Penang ten years ago, had lime-green damask silk and bold phoenix and stork motifs executed in glittering gold thread couchings. It was said to have been ordered from Shanghai some 80 or 90 years ago. Millions of stitches and several miles of gold and silver threads must have gone into the fabrication of this enormous embroidered panel. This hefty pile of gold-thread stitchings on damask silk weighed over 20 pounds.

Another impressive example of large embroidered panels, was a set of frontal drapes formerly used for decorating a red-and-gold Straits Chinese wedding bed in the Penang State Museum, and which was reputedly donated by the descendants of a certain 'Kapitan Chung', of Prince of Wales Island (the early name for Penang).[21] Two vast and impressive golden dragons (one on each side of the panels) are emblazoned on a red background of damask silk. The dragon motifs shown on these drapes were, however, exceptional in embroidery made to Straits Chinese specifications. However, since Kapitan Chung was a wealthy and influential community leader in Georgetown during the latter part of the nineteenth century (?), he probably applied to the imperial office for Overseas Chinese affairs (upon payment of a handsome fee, of course) for the privilege to use the dragon robe (long pao) with the mandarin square emblazoned on the chest to signify official ranking.

With the right to wear the Manchu long pao (of which more later) Kapitan Chung was also permitted to use the emblem of the four-clawed, or mang dragon on other ceremonial objects made for his personal use – the five-clawed imperial dragon motif was, however, reserved for the Emperor and his family. That was probably how the golden dragons came to be used on the drapes of the wedding bed in the Penang State Museum.

Altar hangings which drape ancestral altar tables are usually of two types: the first type consists of a rectangular (or almost square) panel between three- and three-and-a-half feet long and two feet six inches high. These embroidered panels of scarlet red and deep maroon silk fabrics are made in two parts, a narrow, upper rectangular panel about seven or eight inches wide running across its entire length, and lower but broader panel extending from the bottom of the top panel all the way down to the base, and almost touching the floor. This larger of the two embroidered panels contains the main decorative motifs on the altar hanging.

As most of the embroidered altar hangings found in old Straits Chinese homes were made to commemorate weddings or grand birthdays of some patriarchs, the background silk fabric had to be red, while the decorative designs consist mainly of peonies and phoenixes, quails, mandarin ducks and lotuses (symbols representing conjugal fidelity, marital happiness and fertility) and/or storks, cranes, antelopes and bats (symbols of longevity and good fortune). See fig. 49.

The second and bigger type of altar hangings, usually over six feet long and up to three feet six inches high, were meant for the larger of the two ancestral altar tables. Embroidered panels of this type are also designed in the same manner, with a narrow upper panel slightly overlapping a broader but larger panel below.

The decorative motifs are also similar and executed in a combination of satin stitches (of coloured silk threads) and gold thread couchings set against a background of red or maroon silk. Since red is the cardinal colour of all festive and ceremonial objects used by the Chinese, it is pertinent to state that red stood for happiness and good luck. Likewise, the lavish use of gold threads in Chinese embroidery was not merely intended for their showy effects, but more importantly for their symbolic significance in indicating wealth, durability, purity and great virtue (see fig. 79).

Some altar cloths of late nineteenth and early twentieth century dating, come with an outer border ornamented with small fragments of thin mirrors of between half-an-inch and one inch length. The use of such decorative mirror fragments on Chinese embroidery is probably of Indian or Middle Eastern origin, and the traditional Straits Chinese who were receptive to Hindu-Malay customs, readily accepted embroidery with such gaudy decorations. But mirror fragments are not used in embroidered panels made to conservative Chinese tastes.

Like the other embroidered items mentioned above, bed-covers and drapes for doors, being of massive proportions, demand prodigious labour and needlework skills of a high order. They bear the same decorative designs as those seen in altar hangings, lintel panels, drapes for chairs and wedding beds.

Such large embroidered panels were anything but cheap; and in the days gone by, only the more wealthy Straits Chinese families could afford to own all the embroidered paraphernalia required of a lavish wedding. The less affluent who aspired to enjoy the trappings of wealth without having to spend a modest fortune acquiring these things, had to content themselves with hiring all the essential apparel and appurtenances from specialized agents who cater to their needs.

Embroidered costumes

The last item on the list of embroidered articles refers to ceremonial costumes which the Straits Chinese used for their wedding rituals. These ornate and intricately embroidered garments were all fabricated in China by skilled, professional embroiderers according to designs of antiquated costumes which apparently went out of fashion during the two hundred and fifty years that the Manchus ruled over China, from 1644 to 1908.[22]

The ceremonial garb which the Straits Chinese customarily wore, are of Ming period designs and not of Manchu origin; and for as long as anyone can recall, they have always insisted on wearing Ming style costumes, even after the ruling regime in China had passed from the Mings to the Manchus after 1644. It is a testimony to the ingrained sense of conservatism in the Chinese, that despite two-and-a-half centuries of Manchu rule, they continued to design Ming style official garments for overseas Chinese clients in Southeast Asia, even though the Manchu long pao and other Manchu style robes and garments had long ago officially replaced Ming style robes in China.

The ceremonial robe for the nonya bride consists of a T-shaped garment of enormous proportions reaching a little way below the knees, and a skirt made into two pieces – a frontal panel and a back panel joined together at the waist by strings. The sleeves which are straight-cut are voluminously broad, heavy and long – so long, in fact, that they may extend well beyond the tip of the longest finger.

The nonya bride also wore a broad circular collar made up of between three and four layers of *ju-i* head panels arranged in concentric panels. The spaces inside these *ju-i* head panels are finely embroidered with a bewildering variety of auspicious symbols and naturalistic motifs. This multi-layered collar is so broad that the longest of the *ju-i* head panels covers the shoulders, the chest and the back.

Judging by the voluminous proportions of the bridal costume, one may surmise that such ceremonial costumes were never designed or tailored to fit the bride's body snugly and comfortably. Of the six or seven examples of nonya bridal costumes which I have seen over the years, all of them appeared to have been made in one standard size (what they call 'free size' nowadays) so that a bridal robe which was worn by one bride, could also fit any other bride, whether she happened to be fat or thin, tall or short. In fact, the same bridal costume, if properly kept and preserved, could be used by several generations of brides in the same family, until it wore off and had to be replaced with a new robe, or until the family were to decide that each daughter given away in marriage should possess her own set of bridal robes.

Anyone who has taken the trouble to study the complex patterns of these ceremonial garments will realize at once that the stitching of one of these garments must have required many tedious months of painstaking labour. It is not surprising, therefore, that such embroidered costumes were costly even by the standards of those times. Under such circumstances, dress fashions could not be made to change seasonally or even annually.

Indeed, the designs of the Straits Chinese wedding robes remained unchanged for more than 500 years!

From a stylistic point of view, then, the T-shaped bridal robe is obviously of Ming design. The voluminous proportions of the upper garment and the ample two-piece skirt, the straight, broad sleeves with their characteristic parallel rows of fine embroidered designs and their over-reaching lengths, are all peculiar to Ming period costumes.

On this matter regarding the long and unwieldy sleeves of Ming robes, when the bride donned her ceremonial garments, she was expected to strike a formal pose which required her to fold her hands in front of her, and in so doing, adjust the unwieldy ends of the two sleeves in such a way that one slips into the other (see fig. 82). In this way, the intricate embroidered designs on her sleeves are shown to the greatest advantage. It was not customary for the bride to pose with her arms by her sides, as if she were standing to attention, letting those clumsy sleeves dangle in a ludicrous fashion.

It is interesting to compare the Ming style costumes of the bride with the female official robe worn by Manchu royalty and nobility of the Qing dynasty, from the time of the Emperor Kangxi (1662–1722) to that of the Empress Dowager, Cixi (1861–1908).

The official female Manchu garment, although designed on the same T-shaped pattern, differs from the ample, square-cut female garment of the Ming period, in a number of significant respects. Unlike the garment-and-skirt design of the traditional nonya robe, the female Manchu robe is made in *one* piece, from the shoulder all the way down to the feet.

The design is cut in such a way that it hugs the body very snugly at a point somewhat below the armpit. From there the robe sheers outwards and downwards like an inverted 'V' until it reaches the ground. The Manchu sleeves are also different:

Fig. 82 Wedding photograph of Mr and Mrs Gwee Peng Kwee dated 15 January 1927. While Mrs Gwee's wedding costume was of the standard two-piece T-shaped garment and skirt, ornately embroidered with auspicious wedding motifs, that of Mr Gwee was unusual for its being somewhat obsolete by the fashion of the time, namely, a long-sleeved, ankle-length, Manchu style robe of damask silk without embroidered designs, a conical cap, and Manchu riding boots. Officially, the Qing dynasty ended in 1911, and soon thereafter, overseas Chinese were informed of this fact by the Consular of Overseas Chinese Affairs (in Canton?) who also advised them to discard all vestiges of Manchu customs, including their queues. But traditions die hard, and some of the babas found their ancient traditions appealing. Courtesy of Mr Gwee Thian Hock.

they begin broadly at the armpit region and then taper towards the wrists, where they flare out again in the form of crescent-shaped cuffs to cover the upper parts of the hands. These were known as *mati chen* or 'horse-hoof cuffs'.

Now the peculiar characteristics of the Manchu robe, namely, its body-fitting upper parts, its flaring bottom slit at the sides and the tight-fitting sleeves, were actually meant to facilitate horse-riding. For the Manchus, more than the sedentary and urbanized Chinese, were a nomadic people who went about regularly on horseback. For this reason, a rider sitting astride a horse's back, has to have a garment which spreads out sufficiently at the lower ends to enable him to ride in comfort. At the same time, the sleeves have to be tight-fitting, leaving his hands free to control the stirrups and to wield weapons during combat.

The overall design of the female Manchu robe was basically similar to that of the male costume, except in the choice of motifs used in the ornamental designs: male robes frequently carried

Fig. 83 This magnificent dragon robe embroidered in silk of imperial yellow (the dynastic colour of the Qing emperors and their consorts) was probably made to be worn by the Emperor Jiaqing (1796–1820) on his wedding day: with the presence of a number of 'Double Happiness' symbols among the standard official symbols, namely, dragons, bats and clouds. According to tradition, the Emperor Jiaqing was a tall and lanky person. Hence the wave-border at the bottom of the imperial robe was broader than usual. From the Palace Museum, Beijing, the People's Republic of China.

designs of dragons and *qilins*, while female costumes were largely embroidered with peonies and phoenixes. Another feature of *pufu* and *qifu* Manchu robes is worth noting: the lower portions of these robes, from the waist-level down, have four slits, two at the sides, one in front and one behind (see fig. 83).

In other respects, such as the motifs and symbols used, there was hardly any difference between Qing period costumes and those of the preceding dynasties, namely, the Ming, the Yuan and Song dynasties. The Manchus, though anxious to preserve their cultural distinctiveness, found it useful to adopt most of the art and auspicious symbols traditionally used by Han Chinese to embellish their ceremonial garments.

There was one thing though which the Manchus had, from the beginning of their dynastic rule, decided they could not adopt on all their official costumes, and that was the colour red (especially the crimson red) – the dynastic colour of the Ming dynasty. According to Cammann,[23] the Manchus considered red to be an unlucky colour and they forbade red robes from being worn in the imperial courts. Instead, yellow was declared the official colour, and for a long time, yellow *long paos* were reserved only for the Emperor, his consort and members of his family. This is not to say, of course, that the Emperor could not wear a red robe if he had wanted to, but he would wear only yellow dragon robes for all state occasions. This is borne out by the surviving official portraits of many of the Qing Emperors now kept in Beijing's Palace Museum.[24]

But to come back to Straits Chinese bridal costume: the voluminous upper garments and ample skirts are, without exception, made of damask silk of a brilliant red. The decorative motifs are invariably executed in gold thread couchings, and they usually depict a large variety of auspicious symbols and naturalistic objects appropriate to weddings, namely, emblems of scholarly accomplishments, peony blossoms, lotuses, phoenixes, cranes, quails, mandarin ducks, butterflies, dragonflies, bats, etc. The designs on those narrow, parallel panels on the broad sleeves are usually stitched in a combination of gold thread couchings and satin stitches of fine, coloured silk threads.

One unusual bridal garment which my wife acquired more than ten years ago in Penang from an eighty-year-old lady, sported a mandarin square on the chest, and my initial impression was that this splendid scarlet garment with its profusion of bird and floral motifs of gold thread couchings, might have been worn by the groom.[25] The skirt was the colour of deep saffron and was beautifully pleated and ornamented with bird and floral motifs in gold thread couchings (see fig. 84).

The groom's costume (also in two pieces) was also probably derived from Ming period designs. It consists of a loose, long and flowing scholar's robe reaching down to the ankle and is split at the sides. It is made of damask silk, usually lime green in colour (it could also be red if the groom's parents so wished) and richly embroidered wtih auspicious wedding symbols in gold thread couchings.

The wedding robe worn by Baba Yap Kim Swee (see fig. 85) sported four graceful goldfish on the lower part of his costume. Over this ankle-length robe the groom also wore a loose, long-sleeved tunic, somewhat like the upper garment of the *baju loksuan*, which reaches up to waist level. It is usually of scarlet red damask silk with ornate embroidered motifs executed in gold thread couchings. Judging by old wedding photographs in private collections, it appears that while all nonya brides were garbed in what we call 'free size' bridal robes, the grooms' costumes were made to order.

I have often wondered why the Straits Chinese had stuck to observing antiquated customs including wearing ceremonial costumes in Ming period designs for their wedding ceremonies, when they could have easily switched to wearing Manchu

Fig. 84 Embroidered bridal robe complete with pleated skirt in apricot red, from an old family heirloom in Penang. Judging by the presence of the mandarin square on the front (and the back) the bride's father was probably a '*guan*' or mandarin official. The sleeves, each of which is ornamented with five bands of ornate embroidery, are heavy. Late nineteenth/early twentieth century. Collection of Mrs Ho Wing Meng.

Fig. 85 The late Mr Yap Kim Swee and his bride Sng Swee Neo are shown here posing for their wedding photograph in front of the groom's ancestral home. Their ceremonial costumes are designed in traditional Chinese style and ornately embroidered with motifs and symbols considered propitious for a wedding. Straits Chinese wedding costumes were mostly designed and stitched by native embroiderers in China. Courtesy of Winnie and Willie Yap.

style robes in keeping with the changing fashions of the time. And there was time enough for switching over to Manchu dress fashions, since the Manchus ruled over China for over two hundred and fifty years. Besides, we know that when many of the wealthy and influential babas were made 'Kapitans' by the Dutch and the British authorities in the Straits Settlements and in Java during the nineteenth century, they did not hesitate to seek recognition of their newfound status with the imperial authorities in China, by applying for permission to wear one of those Manchu dragon robes, complete with mandarin squares, shoulder drape, conical cap and Manchu boots.

The fortunate few who earned the privilege of wearing the Manchu *long pao* were extremely proud to be accorded the honour. But when it came to their wedding ceremonies (and other festive occasions as well) the Straits Chinese insisted that the bride and groom should faithfully garb themselves with costumes specially made in China to traditional Ming period designs. Even the head-dress for the bride, the black velvet or felt cap for the groom, and the embroidered shoes for the bridal couple, were Ming down to the very last detail!

What could be the reason or reasons for this uncompromising adherence to antiquated customs and traditions of a bygone era? Nobody really knows. The fact is, the Straits Chinese have always regarded themselves as the descendants of early Chinese immigrants who came to Malacca and other parts of Southeast Asia, particularly Semarang in Java, and possibly Medan in North Sumatra, at the beginning of the Ming dynasty. Thus, the Straits Chinese culture which evolved over the next two hundred and seventy-six years (the Ming dynasty persisted from 1368 to 1644) was largely based upon the customs and practices of the Chinese during the Ming dynasty, with minor modifications brought about through partial assimilation of local Malay customs.

This Ming Chinese-cum-Malay culture had obviously served the Straits Chinese well for

several centuries; so there was no necessity for them to adapt to the changes which swept through China, when the Manchus displaced the Ming Emperors as legitimate rulers of China. For one thing, Malacca and other parts of Southeast Asia were never directly controlled by the Manchu authorities in China, and were thus unaffected by their reforms. So the old ways of life continued unchanged. The remarkable thing is that Chinese customs (and dress fashions) dating back to the Ming dynasty should be perpetuated in the Straits Chinese community well into the twentieth century – even after the Qing dynasty had collapsed.

Mandarin squares

No description of the Manchu, or for that matter, the Ming official robe, is complete without some comments on the traditional emblem of official ranking, namely the mandarin square.[26] This is because many successful merchants and traders in the Straits Settlements, conservative Chinese and Straits Chinese alike, took to wearing the Manchu *long pao* or dragon robes (they had to pay for the privilege) during the latter part of the nineteenth century.

The official *long pao* was customarily accompanied by an outer jacket or garment, usually fabricated out of plain black silk, called *pufu*, which officials wore over their official robes. The mandarin square, embroidered with patterns of birds or animals executed in gold thread couchings, was attached to the chest and the back of the *pufu*; some of these have survived among the heirlooms of wealthy Straits Chinese families.

The practice of using the mandarin square to indicate official ranking in the Imperial Court, was first introduced by the Mongols in the Yuan dynasty (1278–1368) during the reign of Kublai Khan. However, when the Ming rulers defeated the Mongols and founded the Ming dynasty in 1368, they continued to adopt the Mongol system

Fig. 86 A set of Qing dynasty mandarin squares intended for civil officials: this is indicated by the bird-and-sun motifs with clouds and waves. Mandarin squares meant for military officers sported only animal motifs. The top split-panel was emblazoned on the chest of the black *pufu* garment, while the bottom panel was stitched to the back. All the motifs are embroidered entirely in gold thread couchings. Dimensions: 12 inches square. Late nineteenth century. Author's collection.

of signifying official ranking in the Court, by the use of the mandarin square.

But in 1391, the Ming Emperor Hongwu decreed that the bird patterns on the squares should be restricted to civil officials, while animal patterns be reserved for military officials. There were nine different ranks, both civil and military, in the hierarchy of court officials, and this system of ranking officials continued to be perpetuated by the Manchu rulers of the Qing dynasty for two hundred and fifty years after they had seized power from the Mings.

The Manchus, of course, had their own insignias of official ranking, and these were based principally on the different kinds of beads which they wore on their official caps and hats: thus, all First Order officials wore a rounded ruby button, while the Ninth (and lowest) Order wore a silver button. However, they found it more convenient to adopt the system of indicating official ranking used during the previous dynasty; so in 1652 the Court of Emperor Shunzhi went ahead to adopt the Ming practice of using mandarin squares to designate their hierarchy of Court officials.

The traditional mandarin square (see fig. 86) comes in two identical pieces, one for the chest and one for the back. Each measures 12 inches square. The one intended for the chest is split into two equal pieces down the middle, because the dark *pufu* outer garment is opened down the centre front and split at the lower sides and lower part of the back.

Such mandarin squares, especially those of the nineteenth century, had to be made to special orders. They could not be purchased ready-made, as very few people were privileged to be bestowed with official appointments by the Imperial Court.

During the nineteenth century, overseas Chinese merchants, traders and community leaders who had distinguished themselves in their professions, were permitted to apply to the Imperial Authorities for the title of 'Guan' or official to be bestowed upon them, upon showing proofs of their achievements, as well as upon payment of a handsome fee. And quite a number of successful overseas merchants, traders and Kapitans did, in fact, avail themselves of this privilege and were bestowed official recognition. This explains why Manchu *long pao* (dragon robes), black *pufu* garments and mandarin squares are occasionally encountered among the heirlooms of certain wealthy and well-known Chinese families, including the Straits Chinese.

This practice of seeking imperial patronage continued until the death of Guangxu and the Empress Dowager, Cixi, in 1908, and the proclamation of the Republic of China in 1911 by Sun Yat-sen. Immediately thereafter, all overseas Chinese were instructed to cut off their Manchu queues, and to discard all vestiges of the Qing dynasty including the dragon robe, the *pufu* garment, the mandarin square, the conical hat and upturned cap, Manchu boots, belts and necklaces of jade beads. As a rule of thumb, therefore, we may date all such artefacts as pre-dating 1911.

Several distinguishing features are peculiar to nineteenth-century mandarin squares. Instead of using the seed knot or satin stitch to embroider all the motifs in coloured silk threads, the decorative designs are all executed in bright gold thread couchings. The aim was to give as much shine as possible to these insignias when they glint against the sunlight.

Older Qing period mandarin squares have their designs more naturalistically depicted, but by the nineteenth century the various details including the bird and animal motifs, the auspicious symbols, the clouds, flowers and seawaves were all rendered in a stylized fashion. And they tended to be crowded and more closely packed. In particular, the symbol of the sun was now oriented to the *right side* in the official's square, but positioned to the *left side* on the square worn by his wife (his first wife, that is!); so that when she sat to her husband's right on state occasions, the bird motif on her husband's square would confront the bird motif on her square, thus presenting a balanced effect.

11
Needles, Threads and Fabrics

THE MATERIALS WHICH traditional nonyas used to fabricate all their embroidered works were virtually identical with those used by their counterparts in China. Straits Chinese embroidery is therefore, largely silk-on-silk, although for certain types of articles such as ceremonial wedding belts, *sapu tangan*, caps, collars, wallets, handbags, spectacle cases, head-gear and shoes, French velvet was employed instead of the usual silk backing. The stitching, however, continued to be executed out of silk threads. Whenever gold and silver threads were used, as in the ornamental designs of those crescent-shaped toe-covering of slippers, they were always executed on small embroidered panels.

One of the great attractions of Chinese embroidery is the great sense of affinity between the thread, the fabric, the subtle shadings of the dyes and the techniques of stitchery. Silk, as everybody knows, is a fabric of delicate smoothness woven out of very fine threads. For this reason, no thread is more suited for embroidering upon it than silk itself; while the kind of stitches which brings out the sheen and spidery texture of silk in the best possible light is obviously the satin stitch.

There is no doubt though that stitches which produce knot-like, loop-like, cross-like or mesh-like textures add interest and variety of textures to a piece of embroidery, and such stitches were in fact regularly employed in Chinese embroidery.

But they do not match the satin stitch for its glistening and mellifluous qualities (see fig. 87), especially when floss and drawn threads of 6 to 8-strand thickness are used.

Needles

In order to execute stitchings of such critical fineness, the nonyas had to match these fine floss threads to needles of wire-thinness. Most of the needles I have found in old needle-boxes left behind by some bygone generations of nonyas some sixty to eighty years ago, turned out to be English-made needles although Chinese-made needles ought to have been available with the stock-in-trade of the travelling Chinese haberdasher whom the nonyas referred to as *jarong*.

Most of these extant needles were either Kirby Nephus ultra needles No. 12, or Milward Sharps No. 12 needles. The finest of Kirby Nephus and Milward Sharps were given as No. 13 – embroidery needles were classified in order of fineness from 13 to 1, so that the bigger the number, the finer the needle. Such needles were three centimetres long. Incidentally, the finest of Milward Sharps and Kirby Nephus used to execute delicate satin, chain and seed stitches were identical with those used for stitching, stringing and threading Rocaille beads of 0.5 mm size.

Embroidery needles of these types are so thin and brittle that breakage must have occurred frequently. Indeed, many cylindrical metal containers meant for holding needles were found with lots of broken and rusted needles in them. Needless to say, threading No. 12 embroidery needles is reserved for people with acute eyesight, while stitching infinitesimal stitches of the types shown in figs. 52, 54 & 57 calls for acute eyesight and very nimble fingers. If we go by some rule-of-thumb datings for most extant pieces of embroidery found in old Straits Chinese homes, those pieces showing stitches of the finest quality went out of production at least seventy years ago.

Threads

Concerning the kinds of threads used in both Chinese and nonya embroidery, silk threads traditionally produced in China were of two types, floss and braided threads. At least eight separate strands of fibres unwound by boiling, stirring and extracting the individual strands of silk from the cocoon, went to make a single strand of silk. For threads of greater thickness and tensile strength, ten, twelve or up to fifteen strands of fibres from separate cocoons have to be wound together to form one strand of silk threads.

Unlike European silk threads the individual strands derived from the cocoons do not have to be glued together. Chinese silk fibres, said to be rich in gluten, adhered to one another quite easily upon being drawn up from the boiling cauldron and reeled into a spool.

Embroidery of the highest quality was always stitched with the finest floss threads which were smooth and luminous. But more than that, much of the beauty of old Chinese embroidery may be attributed to the fact that they produced some of the finest floss silk threads of deep and even colours, with shadings ranging from the darkest to the palest hues.

Dyes

The dyes used for staining the floss and braided silk threads in ancient China were principally derived from the roots, flowers, seeds, stems and saps of various plants. In order to fix such vegetable dyes, Chinese dyers employed mordants derived from other vegetable and mineral substances. Professor Schulyer Cammann[27] has done intensive research on the subject using original Chinese source materials.

Fig. 87 This embroidered panel, 11 inches by 3 inches, with fine and intricate designs, is executed by the use of one principal stitch only, namely, the satin stitch. It represents one of the finest pieces of Straits Chinese embroidery. Probably of late nineteenth or early twentieth century. From Malacca.

For example, the imperial yellow dye was derived from the wood of a thorny tree (*Cudrania triloba*) and the buds of the Japan Pagoda tree (*Sophora japonica*). Golden yellow, however, came from the wood of the sumae tree (*Rhus cotinus*).

Generally, the wood, buds and other parts of a plant are boiled; then, potash from the hemp wood is added as a reagent to fix the colours to the silk threads which are, of course, dipped into the boiling solution for the staining process.

Red dyes were obtained from safflowers, flowers of a certain species of thistle (*Carthanus tinctoris*), the roots of the madder plant (*Rubia cordifolia*) and sapan wood. Again, these substances were boiled with alum and gall-nuts to act as mordants.

Blue dyes came from various sources of indigo 'lantien' or woods. The principal indigo-producing plant was *liao-lan* (*Polygonum tinctorum*), found in Manchuria. Sometimes sapan wood was boiled with the indigo plant to obtain a dark purple blue. Most species of *Indigofera* yield a purple-blue dye.

Black dyes were derived from gall-nuts. (Gall-nuts are actually a kind of growth caused by insects on the leaves of the lacquer tree [*Rhus verniciflua* or *R. sensi-olata*] and acorn nuts of chestnut oak [*Quercus serrata*].)

To produce other colours, Chinese dyers would vary strength of the dye-solution or blend several dyed solutions together. For example, they pro-duced green silks and green threads by first using a yellow dye derived from the buds of *Sophora japonica* and then redyeing by dipping in an indigo solution. Purple dyes were produced by blending blue and red dyes, while brown was derived from the bark of wax myrtle set with ferrous sulphate as the reagent.

Professor Cammann pointed out that while the dyeing of silk fabrics and threads was a fine art of great antiquity, the master dyers in China always kept secret the exact proportions and strengths of the dyeing solution. They usually passed their secrets by word of mouth to their sons or successors and rarely recorded their ideas on paper.

I have elsewhere[28] discussed similar problems connected with Straits Chinese gold and silver-work: master craftsmen usually kept secret the finer points of gold and silver smithing to themselves; and when they and their disciples passed from the scene, their specialized knowledge went with them to the grave. The result was the loss of much valuable knowledge to posterity.

Raw silk threads and silk fabrics dyed with natural vegetable dyes tend to produce colours of softer and purer tones – from the darkest to the lightest hues. One has only to examine old embroideries and tapestries excavated from tombs and desert sands in China, some of which are dated to the Han dynasty (or just over two thousand years) to notice how evenly dyed and subtly shaded the various colours are, despite the passage of time. Remnants of floss silk threads tied in little bundles and left behind in old needle-boxes by a former generation of nonyas, exude a smooth and quiet glow, contrasting rather sharply with the brilliant harshness of silk threads dyed with metallic aniline chemicals.

But even the best of dyes when exposed to light and moisture, fade with passing time (see fig. 81), some more, some less; and even the best preserved pieces mellow and lose their pristine depth and shine. For this reason, old embroideries and even tapestries, should always be kept in places where excessive light is shut out and where the air is relatively dry. Direct sunlight is particularly damaging to natural dyes. Even indirect, reflected sunlight affects the colours of natural dyes adversely within a couple of years of exposure. However, when natural dyes begin to fade, they preserve their original harmony by fading evenly throughout the fabric without leaving unsightly patches and blotches of uneven shades.

Silk fabrics

As for silk fabrics used in traditional embroideries, they can be classified into three principal varieties: those with muslin or gauze-like weaves, those with plain but closely woven texture having a smooth and even sheen, and those with figured and floral motifs of various sorts woven into them. The latter type is known as 'damask silk', the name originally given to silk fabrics with characteristic figured patterns made by weavers in the City of Damascus some two thousand years ago.[29]

Since damask silk costs more than muslin silk or plainly-woven silk, the better pieces of Chinese embroidery were always executed on damask silks. This is not to say, however, that embroideries stitched on plainly-woven fabrics were necessarily inferior; many pieces of excellent workmanship (see figs. 50, 54, 55, 58 & 60) have been embroidered on plain smooth silks.

By and large silk fabrics are very durable, especially when they are carefully preserved from moisture, dampness, insects, direct sunlight, corrosive gases and liquids. As already mentioned in Chapter Four, recent archaelogical findings in China have uncovered painted silk panels and embroidered silk gauzes in an excellent state of preservation dating back to the Western Han dynasty (206 B.C.–A.D. 24).[30]

One reason why these silk fabrics discovered in the coffin of Madam Li Tsang, wife of the Marquis of Tai, a fiefdom in Changsha, Hunan, was so well-preserved, is that the interior of her tomb was found to be thickly lined with lime and charcoal, well-known desiccating agents, which kept the tomb free of moisture for just over two thousand years!

Until these recent findings came to light in 1972, some of the oldest silk fragments in good state of preservation were those which Sir Auriel Stein and Albert von Le Coq found in the desert sands of Central Asia, along the Silk Route. These were dated to the eighth and ninth century A.D. during the Tang dynasty.[31] Thus, at its best, silk fabrics can be made to last two thousand years. But in the damp temperate countries, or worse still, in humid tropical regions, silk deteriorates very rapidly.

Soame Jenyns[32] pointed out that no Chinese embroidery imported into Britain and France during the seventeenth and eighteenth century appeared to have survived, and in the Straits Settlements, no extant Chinese or nonya embroideries in private collections are probably older than a hundred years. In any case, the dating of old embroideries found locally is always based on circumstantial evidence, as no extant pieces are marked and dated after the manner of *nian haos* found in porcelain and paintings.

12
The Story of Silk and Sericulture

SINCE STRAITS CHINESE embroidery is largely silk-on-silk, and represents a long tradition of needlework in China which is lost in the mists of antiquity, it will not be amiss, if I conclude this account by re-telling the story of silk and sericulture as it originated in China. Silk played a most important role in the history of China's trade and political relations with other nations in the Middle East and Europe.

But first, the story of silk and sericulture itself. According to T. H. Tsien,[33] sericulture, or the rearing of the silkworm for spinning silk from its cocoon, was already known in China from the time of the Shang dynasty (1600–1027 B.C.). This is shown by the fact that characters such as *si* (silk), *chan* (silkworm), *bo* (silk articles) and *shang* (mulberry tree) were found inscribed on oracle bones found in Anyang. In fact a preserved cocoon of the silk moth *Bombyx mori* was discovered in neolithic site at Hsi-yin in southern Shanxi, while a silkworm carved out of white jade, 3.15 cm long, was also found in Anyang.

These discoveries indicate that the weaving of silk fabrics was already known in China before historical times. In any case, the Chinese have a legend going back to the time of the Yellow Emperor, Huang Di (reputedly said to have lived between 2698 and 2598 B.C.) according to which, his chief concubine, Lei-tzu of the Hsi-ling clan, was the first person to have reared silkworms,

apparently for the purpose of extracting the silken skeins of the cocoons for weaving silk fabrics. The legend does not actually say that Lei-tzu wore the first piece of silk cloth out of spun silk threads, but only that she was the first person to have reared silkworms. However, Lei-tzu is today worshipped as the patron Goddess of Silk.

By the time of the Zhou dynasty (1027–771 B.C.) the rulers and nobility were already wearing silk robes, and the 'Ode of Pin', a poem dated to between the eighth and seventh century B.C. contains descriptions of young women spinning and dyeing silk fabrics in black, yellow and red for the robes of aristocrats.

In the *Analects* of Confucius (a Zhou period work) there are many references to silk, including one passage which intimated that 'the Master' (Confucius himself) was found to be wearing silk pants![34] It seems evident, therefore, that by about the eighth or seventh century B.C., the Chinese had probably learnt the secret of unwinding the silk cocoon from end to end to obtain a continuous skein of silk measuring between 500 and 1,000 yards long. But of this, more presently.

Traditionally the species of silk moth which is cultivated for its eggs is *Bombyx mori*. These tiny eggs are laid in early spring, but the Chinese collect them and put them in a cold place where the eggs are chilled to prevent them from hatching until about the last week of April. They are then taken out and incubated for ten days. Incidentally, each female moth lays about 500 eggs.

At the end of this time, the eggs hatch out into tiny worms, and they are then transferred to bamboo baskets. They are then immediately fed with finely chopped fresh leaves obtained from the white mulberry tree at half-hourly intervals during the day. From then on, until the silkworms develop into the chrysalis stage about twenty-three days later, they must be fed and cared for regularly under special conditions which are said to be conducive for their healthy development.

To this end, the silkworms must be reared in a pleasant environment – free from excessive noise and smoke, obnoxious smells, strong winds and strong sunlight. They should not be exposed to rain or too much heat or cold: otherwise these supposedly finicky creatures will not produce silk of good quality. They must also be protected from wasps and hornets which could bite and sting them into a state of semi-torpor.

When the silkworms are ready to spin their cocoons, the feeding of mulberry leaves is cut down very drastically. The worms are transferred to trays of rice-straw and a low heat is kept up to stimulate the formation of the cocoons.

Chinese silk farmers have found through long experience, that an exclusive diet of freshly chopped leaves from the mulberry tree was most suitable for the developing caterpillars of *Bombyx mori*, as it stimulated the chrysalis to spin out cocoons of even sheen and smooth texture. This contrasts markedly with the cocoons produced by the wilder species of silk moths: the silken skeins derived from wild cocoons are either greyish, coarse and dull, or greyish, coarse and over-glossy, apparently because the more hardy silkworms of the wild moth feeds on a more varied diet of wild vegetation including wild mulberry and oak leaves.

Silk from wild cocoons were therefore unsuitable for the weaving of high-quality silk demanded by the Court and the mandarin class in China.

However, catering to the finicky appetite of the various species of *Bombyx* silkworms found in different parts of China, required the cultivation of extensive plantations of several species of mulberry trees. The greatest silk-producing region of China was concentrated in Zhejiang, Jiangsu and Anhui. At the end of about twenty-three days, the silkworms would have grown to about three inches or more. During this period they molt several times. But between the nineteenth and twenty-third day, they cease to feed, and soon begin to spin out their cocoons.

The spinning is completed within three days, and during this period they spin out a length of filament which is close to one thousand yards long! The maturing silkworms are now in the chrysalis stage, and if nothing is done to them, fully-grown adult moths would emerge from the cocoons by eating their way out, ten days from the time the spinning started. Soon after they emerge, the female moths will begin to lay their eggs, and when this is completed, they die – all in one day.

The secret of Chinese sericulture

The secret of Chinese sericulture – and it was a secret which the Chinese was said to have successfully kept to themselves for over five hundred years, until it was 'stolen' from them at the beginning of the Christian Era – was how to reel off the silken filament from the cocoon before the adult moth bit its way out. For once the moth has broken through the cocoon, it is impossible to unwind the skein of silk from end to end.

Somewhere in the long history of silk, the Chinese hit upon the solution: they threw the cocoons containing the live chrysalis into a cauldron of boiling water a day or two after the spinning of the cocoon has been completed. The heat in the water killed the chrysalis and dissolved

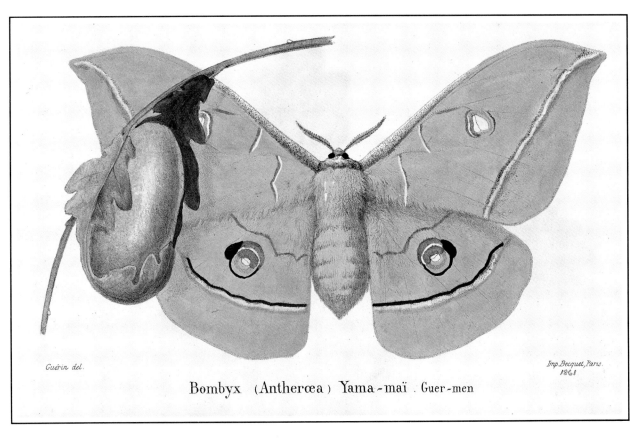

Bombyx (Antherœa) Yama-maï. Guer-men

Guérin del.

Imp.Becquet,Paris.
1861

Fig. 88 The *Bombyx antheroea*, as this 1861 hand-painted engraving shows, is among the largest and most impressive species of silk-producing moths native to parts of China and Mongolia. However, the quality of fabric that can be spun out of its cocoon is a coarse variety of silk, known as tussah silk, expensively imported into Europe for many centuries. Tussah silk does not have the mellifluous smoothness and sheen of Chinese silk derived from *Bombyx mori*. Incidentally, the silkworm of *Bombyx antheroea* can thrive on oak leaves. Author's collection.

the sericin, a glue-like substance produced by the silkworm to bind the cocoon together.

Having done this, the next step was to use a small rush-broom with fine twigs (a bamboo comb, it was found, would do just as well) to beat very lightly at the boiling mixture in the cauldron. This caused some of the loosened silk skeins to adhere to the twigs and unravel the cocoons in the process. Chinese silk workers found that they could draw out those filaments adhering to the rush-broom (eight, ten or twelve filaments at a time) and slowly lead them to a reeling machine where they are twisted into a single thread.

Very early in the development of silk, the Chinese found that the winding of several filaments of silk to form one thread could be effected straight away as they left the boiling cauldron without having to glue them together. In the beginning the Chinese must have found that the first several yards of threads coming out of the cauldron were too fluffy and flossy; so these were discarded.

This, then, was the 'secret' which silk weavers in Central Asia, the Middle East and Europe wanted to learn from the Chinese. It had nothing to do with the charming but apocryphal story told by the famous Chinese Buddhist pilgrim, Hsuan Tsang, of the Tang dynasty, about a wily stratagem which a certain Prince of Khotan hatched to smuggle the eggs of *Bombyx mori* out of China to his Central Asian city.

According to Hsuan Tsang, then, the Prince had written to the Emperor of China during the Han dynasty to ask for the hand of one of his daughters in marriage, saying that such a marriage would help cement a firm political alliance between China and the Kingdom of Khotan. At the same time, the wily prince had written another confidential letter addressed to his bride-to-be, saying that life in Khotan could be pretty dreary compared to life in China, because she would not be able to pass her leisure hours weaving silk and stitching lovely embroideries.

He then hinted very strongly, that if she intended to spend her life in Khotan in a meaningful way, it might not be a bad idea to consider smuggling the eggs of the silk moth in a secret pouch hidden in her elaborate head-dress. According to the legend, the gullible princess was only too glad to comply; so it was that she hid some *Bombyx* eggs in her head-dress and brought them some three thousand miles west to the City of Khotan.

Apparently, this story has become a permanent part of the folklore of Khotan; for among the various interesting artefacts which Western archaeologists recovered in their expeditions to Central Asia, was a pottery tile depicted with the portrait of a woman with an elaborate head-dress. The accompanying inscriptions with a hand pointing at her hair, intimated that silkworm eggs were hidden in the folds.

The City of Khotan has, since the end of the Han dynasty, maintained its reputation as a centre of silk-weaving in Central Asia. But whether the silk industry in that remote oasis was founded by a plucky Chinese princess who carried silkworm eggs in her head-dress all the way from Changan, is quite another matter.

Roman history is also replete with legends about how the eggs of the silk moth *Bombyx mori* and the art of sericulture was brought from China (known as 'Serinda') – first to Constantinople, the eastern capital of the Roman Empire, and from there to Italy and France, during the fifth and sixth century A.D. According to Procopius (in his *De Bello Gothico IV*) Emperor Justinian had been greatly irked by the enormous drain of gold and silver from Constantinople caused, he was informed, by the great consumption of silk fabrics for making expensive robes and garments for his officials and the wealthy merchant class.

Since the silk trade was held in the hands of the Persian traders, the prices of silk were exorbitant. Justinian was therefore interested to find a way of reducing his dependence on Persian traders by

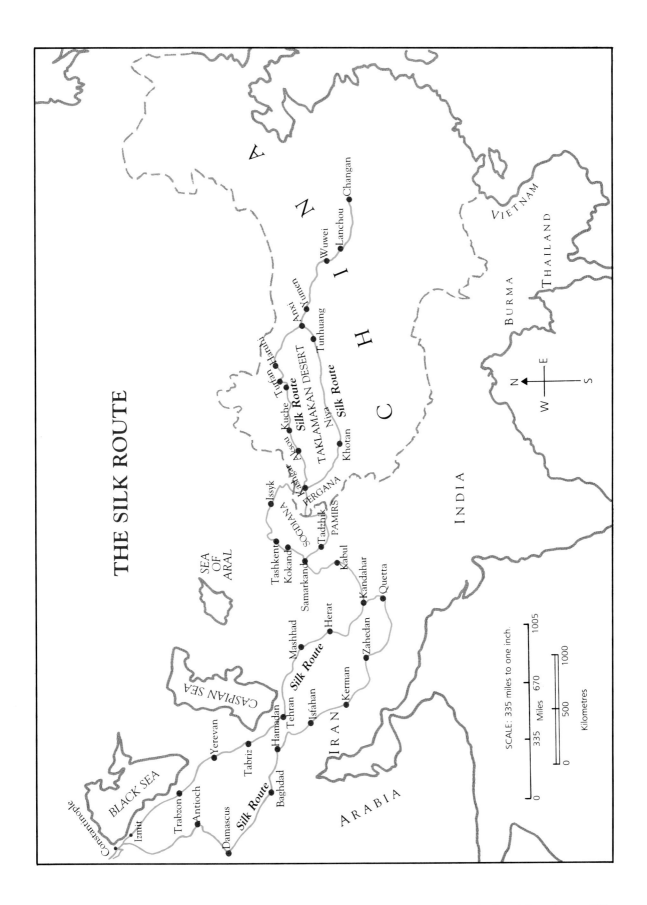

THE SILK ROUTE

SEA OF ARAL

CASPIAN SEA

BLACK SEA

Constantinople

Izmit

Trabzon

Antioch

Damascus

Silk Route

Baghdad

Tabriz

Yerevan

Hamadan

Tehran

Isfahan

Silk Route

Kerman

Mashhad

IRAN

Herat

Zahedan

Kandahar

Quetta

Kabul

Tashkent

Kokand

Samarkand

SOGDIANA

Tadzhik

PAMIRS

FERGANA

Issyk

Kashgar

Aqsou

Kuche

Turfan

Hami

Silk Route

Anxi

Yumen

Tunhuang

Silk Route

TAKLAMAKAN DESERT

Niya

Khotan

A N

C H I

Wuwei

Lanchou

Changan

VIETNAM

BURMA

THAILAND

INDIA

ARABIA

N
E
S
W

SCALE: 335 miles to one inch.

335   670   1005

Miles

0   500   1000

Kilometres

0

The Story of Silk and Sericulture   155

setting up a silk-weaving industry in Constantinople.

Procopius recounted that when certain monks from the land of the 'Indians' heard about Justinian's problem, they came to offer help. 'They said they had lived a long while in a country where many nations of the Indians (?) and which was called *Serinda*, and had learnt the whole art of sericulture. When the Emperor had promised sufficient reward, they returned to India (?) and then smuggled the eggs from which they proceeded to hatch the silkworms and put them out on mulberry leaves.'[35]

Theophanes, another writer, repeated the same story but said that the eggs of *Bombyx mori* were smuggled to Constantinople by Nestorina monks in a hollow bamboo cane. Like all legends, these stories contain a mixture of fact and fiction.

The factual part of it is, of course, that by the sixth century, the secrets of Chinese sericulture were already known in Constantinople, and silk farmers there had created a thriving industry in silk-weaving which brought wealth and prosperity to its people and government. The fictional aspect of these stories concerns the legend of smuggled moth-eggs.

I have often wondered at the myth perpetuated by many Western writers and historians, namely, that the secrets of Chinese silk, and more importantly, the art of sericulture, had been brought to Europe in the form of some smuggled eggs of the *Bombyx* moth. This story is obviously untrue, because in normal circumstances, moth eggs hatch within ten days after they have been laid, unless they are carefully chilled for, say, several weeks at the most, to prevent them from hatching, until the weather is sufficiently warm and conducive to the growth of the silkworms.

Now the long caravan journey by camels from the old imperial capital in Changan (or Xian as it is known today) to Damascus, across vast, inhospitable deserts, dangerous mountain passes, long detours and pauses along the way, lasted up to three years or more. It is doubtful if the moth eggs could have survived the vicissitudes of that difficult journey even under the best conditions.

In order for this story to gain sufficient credence, some historians would have to explain how sericulturalists, planning to smuggle the eggs of the silk moth out of China, eventually hit upon the idea of keeping the eggs of *Bombyx mori* frozen throughout the entire 7,000-kilometre journey from Changan to Constantinople.

They would have to show, moreover, that these sericulturalists succeeded in inducing the frozen eggs to hatch into live caterpillars at the end of that long and difficult journey. No mention of this essential technical feat, however, is reported in any of the various accounts of the development of the silk industry in Europe, that I have read so far — from Procopius to Boulnois. Instead, all available accounts about the 'smuggled' eggs of *Bombyx mori*, seemed to have conveniently glossed over this difficulty by relying upon the mystique of this fanciful story to overcome the obvious technical problems connected with preserving the moth eggs in a state of suspended animation for several years at a stretch.

Besides, the impression suggested by this colourful story, is that the *Bombyx* moth was found only in China, and therefore had to be brought out at great risks and great expense, because the Chinese authorities were supposedly said to have imposed a rigid embargo against the export of moth eggs for at least five hundred years!

Nothing could be further from the truth. Actually, several species of *Bombyx* moths produce wild silk cocoons of one type or another, and they are not confined within the geographical boundaries of China but found throughout Asia and Europe. In fact, as early as 3000 B.C., weavers in India, Egypt, Persia and Assyria had already known how to weave a variety of coarse silk fabric out of the cocoons of wild silk.

What made Chinese silk so different from other varieties of coarsely spun silk fabrics, was its lightness, its translucency, its lovely sheen and its smooth and consistent texture – qualities which had never been encountered in Europe or the Middle East, until the coming of Chinese silks in these countries.

As for the alleged difficulty of procuring the eggs of the silk moth, contrary to what writers and historians have claimed, nothing could have been easier. After all, sericulture was widely practised throughout China; and in certain provinces such as Jiangsu, Zhejiang and Anhui, practically every household was involved in one or more aspects of the silk industry. As for the moth eggs, they were available by the billions!

What about the allegation concerning the secretiveness of the 'inscrutable orientals' who cunningly concealed the techniques of sericulture from the prying eyes of foreigners? The truth of the matter is that sericulture in China had always been a cottage industry, and its trade 'secrets' had been known to millions of householders at any given time for at least three thousand years.

Sericulture was, at no time, a state monopoly rigidly controlled by the Imperial Court in Chang-an, and its methods of production were not closely guarded secrets. How could they be, since the silk industry was engaged by so many people scattered over such an enormous country? Even assuming that some of the more zealous of Chinese officials had tried, from time to time, to cast a cloak of secrecy and mystery over the silk industry in China, their efforts would have been futile.

Hence, if the techniques of sericulture took such a long time to reach the West, it was in all likelihood not the doings of the Chinese, but the machinations of the Persian, Syrian and Turkish traders and middlemen who made vast profits by supplying Chinese silks to the lucrative markets of the Roman Empire.[36] They, more than anybody else, had a vested interest in preventing knowledge of Chinese sericulture from being disseminated to Europe.

In any case, silk was bound to be an expensive commodity, because it had to be transported by overland, camel caravan from Serinda (the Latin name for China) to the Roman Empire. Until the independent fiefdom of Khotan in the western edge of the Taklamakan Desert began producing its own varieties of raw and finished silks for export to the West, at about the beginning of the Christian Era, this precious fabric had to be carried on camel-back much of the way from Changan, the formal imperial capital, to Constantinople.

Now the distance from Changan to Constantinople, as the crow flies, is in excess of seven thousand kilometres. But in actual fact, large stretches of the old silk route were tortuous, as they wound through perilous mountain passes and inhospitable deserts, from the Gobi to the Taklamakan in Central Asia, through either the Tien Shan Mountains or the Karakoram ranges, into Turkestan and the deserts of Persia, and stretched all the way to Baghdad and Damascus.

From Damascus, raw silk was processed and woven into damask silk before it was sent to Antioch, and from there through Asia Minor to Constantinople. Thus, by the time the original consignment of silk from Changan reached the eastern capital of the Roman Empire, it had already traversed over eight thousand kilometres, and during that time it must have passed through the hands of the Persians, the Turks and the Syrians.

At best, it took several years to complete the long and tortuous overland journey from Changan to Constantinople. And through it all, intrepid and enterprising foreign traders, rather than the Chinese themselves, monopolised the transactions of silk with the Roman Empire. Is it any wonder, then, that silk was worth its weight in gold?

Dating

The reader who has taken the trouble to read the text thus far, will have noticed that I alluded in several places to the dating of most extant pieces of beadwork and embroidery illustrated in this book. I did not, however, specifically discuss the subject of dating in any detail, assuming as I did, that anyone who had grasped the import of the discussion, would have been sufficiently apprised by now, that the various artefacts under consideration are all datable to the end of the nineteenth and the beginning of the twentieth century. I now realize that this assumption may not perhaps be obvious to everyone. Hence, a separate note concerning the methods of dating is necessary, even at the risk of repeating myself.

Like all other categories of cultural artefacts peculiar to the traditional Straits Chinese community, *the various items of beadwork and embroidery shown here are, with very few exceptions, dated to the end of the nineteenth century and the opening decades of the twentieth century.* While it is true that none of the extant pieces of beadwork and embroidery have been signed or dated with the *nian haos* seen in porcelain, for example, we know on circumstantial evidence (e.g. historical evidence, stylistic evidence, and information provided by old Straits Chinese families which once owned these things) that the bulk of Straits Chinese beadwork and embroidery were made, imported or presented between 1880 and 1920. It is also interesting to note that this period also coincided with the era of prosperity enjoyed by the merchant and trading classes in the Straits Chinese community. I have, therefore, avoided appending the words 'late nineteenth/early twentieth century' *ad nauseum*, to each and every descriptive caption.

Difficulty of preservation

No beadwork or embroidery dating to the early nineteenth, or even late eighteenth century have, as far as I know, been authenticated. As for early eighteenth- or seventeenth-century beadwork and embroidery, one can safely say that none has survived to this day. This is not particularly surprising, when one considers what havoc can be wrought to exposed fabrics made from natural fibres, by the warm and humid climate of the tropics, not to mention the unsavoury contributions of mould, mildew, mites, silverfish, cockroaches and mice!

Beadwork and embroidery which are left exposed to damp atmosphere, dust, smoke, fumes and even reflected sunlight, deteriorate very rapidly. For this reason, embroidered altar cloths, panels, banners, buntings and other hangings set up in Chinese temples throughout Singapore and Malaysia, where the internal atmosphere is perpetually enveloped in smoke and fumes from burning joss-sticks, candles, oil-lamps and joss-papers, become so faded, frayed and crumbling, that they have to be replaced with new ones every fifteen or twenty years.

On the other hand, beaded slippers, small embroidered panels and ornaments and embroidered costumes, having been carefully wrapped in dry cotton cloths or soft rice-paper, and deposited in camphor-wood chests or pig-skin chests with sprinklings of dried pepper seeds, maintain their pristine state of freshness and beauty – even after a lapse of seventy or eighty years! But generally speaking, the hot and steamy climate of the tropics is notoriously unfavourable for the preservation of silk, cotton, linen and woollen fabrics.

Circumstantial evidence

As for the methods of dating based on circumstantial evidence, these may be divided into two principal types. Firstly, there is evidence based purely on stylistic characteristics. According to this method of dating, we try to determine the possible age of a piece of antique by looking for certain ostensible features (in the case of beadwork and embroidery, the kinds of beads employed, the kinds of stitches preferred, the kinds of designs depicted, etc.) which may, on independent grounds, be attributed to the workmanship peculiar to some specific period or era.

Secondly, we try to determine the original owners of these artefacts, and then check the records and other sources of information (e.g. birth certificates, registers of associations, clubs or business organizations to which the individuals belonged) concerning their dates of birth and death. We also include under this category of circumstantial evidence, information and testimonies of the person's friends, relatives or direct descendants, which may enable us to date these artefacts.

Stylistic characteristics

As far as Straits Chinese beadwork and embroidery are concerned, attempts to devise an *ad hoc* system of dating based on stylistic considerations, are not particularly useful. This is because stylistic considerations, whatever they may be, are minor. In fact, no significant differences suggesting some kind of evolutionary trend, or widely disparate differences, in techniques and themes, can be detected. To the practised eye though, the features which distinguish a piece of Straits Chinese embroidery from one made in China, are not difficult to make out. But *within* Straits Chinese embroidery, it is not possible to say which piece with what characteristics, belong to what particular period. Most extant articles of nonya needlework are fabricated in what one might call a 'nineteenth-century style'. Even the most astute student of Straits Chinese art would be hard put to say, on stylistic evidence, what a typical eighteenth-century nonya embroidery would look like. Since ingrained conservatism was a distinctive characteristic of the traditional Chinese mind, eighteenth-century nonya

embroidery would, in all probability, show no significant differences in style from nineteenth-century pieces – other things being equal. The same may be said of the alleged differences between late nineteenth-/early twentieth-century beadwork and those of eighteenth-century dating – if any.

Owner information

Where it is not possible to elicit the names of the original owners or families from which these articles were procured, or where stylistic evidence is not of much help, recourse to other forms of circumstantial evidence is necessary. Thus the greater the number of hands through which a piece of antique beadwork or embroidery has passed, the more difficult it is to obtain accurate evidence concerning its origin.

Fortunately for most students and collectors of *Malayana* in Singapore and Malaysia, it is sometimes possible to procure antique beadwork and embroidery directly from old Straits Chinese families through discreet recommendations of friends and acquaintances. Antique *objets d'arts* obtained in this manner are, of course, much easier to date, because information about them and their connections with the family's history is often willingly supplied by some member of the family. As for many antique dealers who often purchase their supplies from elderly nonyas by visiting their homes, it is their custom never to disclose the names or addresses of their vendors, partly because their sources of supplies are regarded as trade secrets, and partly because they have given a solemn undertaking not to embarrass their highly sensitive vendors, by divulging their names to potential buyers of their wares.

Occasionally, however, a dealer would deliberately 'leak' out information by hinting that such-and-such articles came from one of the descendants (names not given) of some well-known personalities from the late nineteenth and early twentieth century, such as the Tan Kim Seng family in Singapore and Malacca, the Khoo and the Chung families in Penang, the Yap Ah Loy family of Kuala Lumpur, the Seah Liang Seah family of Singapore, and so on. The purpose of this deliberate 'leakage' is that of pure profit – not, of course, an open betrayal of confidence, for the anonymity of his vendors is preserved, nor for that matter, an accidental disclosure of some closely guarded trade secret, for the sources of his supplies remain undisclosed. For if a dealer can capitalize upon the reputation of some well-known personalities, it simply means he can charge higher prices for 'treasures' associated with such personalities! However, if the dealer is in fact telling the truth, namely, that some pieces of beadwork and embroidery he is offering for sale, once belonged to some well-known Straits Chinese families, then checking the relevant dates in the records of the *kongsis* or clan associations, presents no insuperable difficulties. By and large, it is true to say that the sale of antiques by old-fashioned babas and nonyas is often shrouded in secrecy.

By contrast, the sale and disposal of antiques and works of art which formerly belonged to some aristocratic families in Britain and Europe, is often advertised internationally by various auction houses on behalf of the original owners or members of their families. This is because considerable prestige is often attached to works of art associated with the names of prominent royalty and nobility; and the prospects of obtaining higher bids are greater than if the articles in question had belonged to some unknown and untitled individuals – unless, of course, the works of art turn out to be items of great rarity, or were fabricated by historically famous craftsmen or artists.

This practice of giving public notice to the sale of antiques which once belonged to some European aristocratic families is, however, greatly frowned

upon in Chinese customs, Straits Chinese not excepted. Indeed, the more famous the owner of some antique works is, the more discreet he or his descendants must be, about his desire to dispose of some of his treasured family heirlooms. Hence, to make public one's intention of selling away one's family heirloom was customarily regarded as a terrible *loss of face* which no respectable Chinese gentleman would tolerate, if he could help it. To the Chinese way of thinking, the public disposal of one's family heirloom was a disgrace to the good name and reputation of one's ancestors, because it was tantamount to an open admission that one was broke. For this reason, when the descendants of former generations of Straits Chinese families were forced to dispose of their family antiques for one reason or another, the Straits Chinese conducted all their transactions with antique dealers in secret, and only through the back doors of their houses, as it was considered *malu* (shame) or *main bangsat* (i.e. cheating, or not observing accepted customs) to let their neighbours know that they were selling away their family's properties.

Fortunately for the student of Straits Chinese heritage, the lack of accurate information concerning the original ownership of some antique artefact, is not a matter of great significance. For as already pointed out before, most of the important cultural artefacts of Straits Chinese origin (e.g. porcelain) cannot be dated earlier than the beginning of the nineteenth century. It is true that the history of the Straits Chinese community in Malacca can be traced as far back as the beginning of the fifteenth century. But, except for some faded and worn-out inscriptions on several tombstones in Bukit China, Malacca, some of the most notable mementoes of this remarkable community (e.g. their houses) belong to the late eighteenth and early nineteenth century. Where beadwork and embroidery are concerned, extant pieces are of more recent origin, namely, late nineteenth century.

Notes

1. *Civilization: A Personal View.* London: B.B.C. and John Murray, 1969. Chapter 1, p. 1.

2. In Malacca, particularly, the racial riots of 1969 tended to polarize the people there into Chinese or Malay; and the Straits Chinese in Malacca who were neither 'Chinese' nor 'Malay' in the cultural and linguistic senses of these terms, were therefore caught in the crossfire. The Straits Chinese in Penang had no such problem because they all spoke a brand of Hokkien which was peculiar to Penang. Baba Malay was spoken at home, but it was not the *lingua franca* of Georgetown.

3. In the 1940s, Dr Mathew Stirling of the Smithsonian Institution, discovered in Cerro de las Mesas 782 priceless jade carvings, among which were at least half a dozen necklaces made of jade beads. Alberto Ruz Lhuiller discovered in the Maya pyramid of Palenque, the skeleton of a royal person inside an enormous carved sarcophagus wearing a death mask of green jadeite and several green necklaces made of jade beads. In Olmec, Toltec, Maya and Aztec cultures in Central and South America, jade was a precious stone reserved only for the nobility.

4. *Jewels of the Pharaohs.* New York: Ballantine Books, 1978.

5. *Ur of the Chaldees,* final account revised by P. R. S. Moorey. London: Herbert Press, 1982.

6. Van der Sleen, in his *A Handbook of Beads,* reported that Quaritsch Wales found carnelian, amethyst and quartz beads near Ayuthia in Thailand. In Johore Llama, Gardner found black glass beads which are said to be of Phoenician or Syrian origin. Carnelian, quartz, and red and green jasper beads were also recovered in the ruins. These beads are said to date back to the beginning of the Christian era, although Johore Llama was founded only in the sixteenth century.

7. It was Tome Pires, in his *Suma Oriental,* who first mentioned that the early Chinese traders in Malacca married Malay girls of Sumatran or Javanese descent; their local spouses could then help to look after their shops whenever they went on business trips to China and other parts of Southeast Asia. This practice of marrying local Malay girls was, however, discontinued when Muslim girls were prohibited from marrying non-Muslim Chinese traders – and most of the traders from Fujian province were obviously non-Muslims. Pires did say, however, that the Chinese traders took to marrying girls of Bugis and Balinese extraction.

In any case, this story about the Straits Chinese as descendants of Malay and Chinese ancestors has been repeated by various historians who have commented on the origins of the Straits Chinese. However, quite a number of Malacca babas have Indian blood in them. These are the 'chettiars' of Malacca, descendants of South Indian immigrants who settled in Malacca a long time ago, and who married Chinese girls from the Straits Chinese community, mainly because the Chinese were non-Muslims and thus, more liberal in their customs and practices. It would seem, therefore, that the Straits Chinese, especially the ones from Malacca, come from a multi-racial background.

8. Representative examples of such beaded artefacts may be seen in the collections of Muzium Negara in Kuala Lumpur and the Tun Abdul Razak Muzium in Kuching, Sarawak.

9. Ho Wing Meng, *Straits Chinese Silver*. Singapore: Times Books International, 1984. Chapter 1.

10. See May and Geoffrey Payton's *The Observer's Book of Glass*, London: Frederick Wayne & Co., 1976, and L. Uresova's 'Glass' in *The Pictorial Encyclopedia of Antiques*, London: Hamlyn, 1970, for useful information on glass and glass-making techniques.

11. *New Archaeological Finds in China*. Peking: Foreign Language Press, 1973.

12. Mr Peter Wee of Katong Antique House, Singapore, owns a splendid collection of over seventy pairs of antique *kasut manek*, which I have been privileged to handle and examine closely at leisure. Most of them are in a pristine state of preservation, even though the most recent are at least 50 years old. The majority are said to have come from Penang. However, none of the beaded and embroidered slippers is older than 90 years. But one cannot be too sure about the dating of these slippers because they do not bear date marks at all. Dating is largely based on information provided by antique dealers who purchased their artefacts directly from private homes.

13. See *Straits Chinese Silver*, pp. 80–86.

14. Op. cit., p. 6.

15. See Ho Wing Meng, *Straits Chinese Porcelain*. Singapore: Times Books International, 1983.

16. The first European to mention Chinese silk, silk-weaving and embroidery was apparently Aristotle at the time of Alexander the Great (356–323 B.C.). But there was no regular contact between China and Europe until the beginning of the Christian era. Dionysius Periegetes, a Greek monk, commented that the 'Seres' (i.e. the Silk-people) made garments of a fineness rivalling spider webs; and another ancient Greek writer Strabo recounted that during one of their warring expeditions into Asia (he did not say where in Asia) they saw their enemies dressed in magnificent robes embroidered with silk and gold threads, and the Greeks were greatly impressed by the beauty of these robes. When Alexander the Great captured the magnificent royal tent of Darius after a pitch battle, he was so impressed with the sheer splendour of Darius's robes of silk and gold threads that he ordered his Cypriots attendants to make him some robes designed in the same style.

The Romans who replaced the Greeks as the masters of Europe, Asia Minor and North Africa, soon became addicted to the use of silk for their official garments. But up to about A.D. 400, only the nobility and provincial governors could afford to wear silk. Virgil wrote ecstatic poems in praise of silk, while the stern Seneca, a Roman senator, condemned the use of revealing silk garments as lewd and indecent. 'Such clothes,' Seneca remarked sarcastically, 'if we can call them clothes at all, afford no degree of protection to the body or to the modesty of the wearer.' In his opinion, 'no woman could swear that she was not naked'! (See L. Boulnois, *The Silk Road.*)

17. According to Soame Jenyns (See *Chinese Art* Vol. 3. New York: Rizzoli, 1981) Yuan Shih-kai told his friends that he spent £2,500 on his wardrobe of various dragon robes and official garments when he was appointed Viceroy of Korea; and £2,500 at the turn of the present century was an enormous sum of money.

It was unlikely, of course, that a wealthy Straits Chinese family would spend even the equivalent of a thousand pounds (or up to twenty thousand Singapore dollars today) on embroidered garments and articles in those days. But when one recalls that embroidered articles required for an elaborate wedding celebration included several heavily embroidered garments for both the bride and groom, the bridesmaid, the groom's attendant, parents of the bride and groom, not forgetting valances, drapes for doors and windows, the wedding bed, wedding chairs, door panels, altar cloths, banners, embroidered lanterns, ceremonial umbrellas, bed-covers, etc., one can appreciate the heavy costs involved. If the Straits Chinese had rented all these appurtenances from the various hiring agencies, they would only have to pay a fraction of the costs.

18. I have often wondered at the complete lack of interest for Rocaille beads on the part of the Chinese, both native and overseas Chinese (the Straits Chinese being an exception). When the Portuguese traders (and subsequently the Dutch and English traders) sailed their galleons up to the ports of Macau and Canton early in the sixteenth century, they must have brought large crates of coloured glass beads with them to barter for tea, porcelain and silk with the Chinese. After all, glass beads had been eagerly accepted by the natives of Africa, Southeast Asia, Micronesia and Polynesia, while faience and other types of semi-precious stone beads had been the standard stock-in-trade of the early Arab and Indian traders.

Apparently the Chinese must have rejected these glass beads as articles of worthless value, for despite four hundred years of trading relations between China and the European nations, Rocaille beads do not feature in garments and decorative articles fashioned by Chinese artisans for home consumption or for export overseas. This is not surprising because the Chinese, from a very early period in their history, had already learnt how to fashion beads out of various materials, and while beads and beaded ornaments did not feature prominently in their culture, they were certainly available. For their nobility, the Chinese preferred beads fashioned out of jadeite, lapis-lazuli, turquoise, coral and pearls. By comparison, Rocaille beads were worthless baubles.

The Straits Chinese are unique in being the only community of *huaqiao* or overseas Chinese, who took a fancy to Rocaille beads and developed a special craft of beadwork which has now become a distinguishing cultural trait of their community. But this is because the Straits Chinese culture is made up of part-Malay and part-Chinese customs and traditions.

19. Not all of these embroidered (and tapestry) panels framed with broad, brocaded borders are newly made products. During the period of the 'Great Proletarian Cultural Revolution' (from about 1965–75) many of the embroidered panels and fragments of tapestries exported out of China, were actually fragments of needlework cut out of various parts of old embroidered dragon robes and other official garments, altar cloths, etc. They are probably of nineteenth century dating.

20. See *Straits Chinese Silver*, Chapter 4.

21. When Malaysia attained political independence, or 'Merdeka', from Britain on 31st August 1957, the name of Penang Island was changed to 'Pulau Pinang'. The Malay word *pinang* stands for 'areca nut', and 'Pulau Pinang', therefore, means 'Island of Areca nuts', which it supposedly was in times gone by.

22. The Nelson Gallery of Art in Kansas City, Minneapolis, USA, probably owns the largest single collection of Chinese Imperial robes of the Qing dynasty, dating from Shunzhi (1644–62) to Xuantong (1908–11). Most of these robes were said to have been acquired by Laurence Sickman who happened to be in China during the last tumultuous years (i.e. 1940–48) of the Chinese Civil War when the Communists under Mao Tse-tung were winning the war against the Kuomintang led by Chiang Kai-shek.

23. See page 14 of his *China's Dragon Robes*. New York: Ronald Press, 1952.

24. Note the magnificent photographs (in colour) of Qing emperors and their empresses in *Life of the Emperors and Empresses in the Forbidden City*. 2d ed. with English captions. Beijing: City Travel and Tourism Press, 1983.

25. In Queeny Chang's *Memories of a Nonya* (Singapore: Eastern Universities Press, 1981), there are several black and white photographs of her wedding costume (both the inner and outer garments) with a similar mandarin square embroidered on the front. According to nonya Chang, the emblem of the square is that of a silver pheasant, indicating the Fifth Order of official ranking in the Manchu Court. Nonya Chang was entitled to wear the mandarin square because her father Tjong Ah Fie was a wealthy and influential Chinese community leader in Medan, Sumatra, who had been honoured with the title of 'Kapitan' by the Dutch Colonial Administrators for his contributions to community welfare.

26. Dr S. Cammann has made a detailed and learned study of Mandarin Squares based on Chinese literary sources. It is published under the title of 'Chinese Mandarin Squares', *University of Pennsylvania Museum Bulletin*, Vol. 17, 1953.

27. See his *China's Dragon Robes*. New York: Ronald Press, 1952.

28. Ho Wing Meng, *Straits Chinese Silver*. Singapore: Times Books International, 1984.

29. No one knows when skilled Syrian weavers in the City of Damascus invented the method of weaving silk fabrics by incorporating floral and foliated patterns into their texture. Tradition has it that by about the beginning of the Christian era, the weavers in Damascus had begun exporting damask silk to other parts of the Middle East, Africa and Europe. For more than five hundred years thereafter, the Syrian weavers

dominated the market for damask silk. However, when the Muslim hordes poured out of the Arabian deserts in the seventh century A.D. in their quest for conquest and religious conversion, the Syrian weavers fled Damascus and carried their trade and industry to Greece.

30. See Part I in *New Archaeological Finds in China*. Peking: Foreign Languages Press, 1974.

31. Sir Auriel Stein reported finding a large cache of silk fabrics (well-preserved) in graves at Lon-lan in the Tarim Basin. But there were no embroidered silks other than tapestries in these findings. In the Caves of a Thousand Buddhas in Tunhuang, Sir Auriel did, however, find a rare and enormous silk panel measuring nine feet long by six feet wide. It depicts the buddha with four attendants in life-size, and all the figures were executed in solid satin stitches over a linen background. It is dated to the eighth century and is now kept in the British Museum.

32. *Chinese Art*, Volume 3. New York: Rizzoli, 1981. Chapter on textiles, pp. 30–31.

33. Tsien, T. H. *Written on Bamboo and Silk*. Chicago: The University of Chicago Press, 1962.

34. In chapter VI, line 9 of the *Analects*, we read of Confucius that 'his undergarments, except when it was required to be of the curtain shape, was made of silk (*ssu*) cut narrow at the top and wide below.' James Legge's translation.

35. Procopius. *De Bello Gothico*, IV, p. 17. Incidentally, while Justinian upbraided his court officials and ministers for their extravagant habit of wearing expensive silk robes, he and his wife Theodora wore the finest silk robes for the inauguration of Haggia Sophia, the greatest of Byzantium basilica in A.D. 537.

36. On this point, it should also be noted that among the merchants, traders and caravaners who were actively engaged in purveying silk between China and the Roman Empire, from the Han to the Tang dynasty (i.e. from about 206 B.C. to A.D. 700) was a race of largely forgotten people, namely, the 'Sogds' or 'the Sogdians'. The Sogdians are believed to have originated from Central-west Asia in the region around Samarkand and Bokhara, south of the Aral Sea. That region was known in ancient times as 'Sogdiana'. The Chinese called it 'the land of the Kans'.

Racially (if one may judge by Han and Tang period pottery statues of camel-drivers and foreign merchants on camelback), they were a tribe of Indo-European origin, with long, thin faces, prominent noses, deep-set eyes and bushy beards. They were not unlike the Uighurs and the Uzbeks who now live in Kazakhstan in Soviet Russia and Western China.

During the heyday of the Sogdiana era (from about the first to the seventh century A.D.) the Sogdians constitute a district nation with a language, a distinctive written script, a religion (largely Zoroastrianism) and a culture of their own. They also founded settlements all along the silk route stretching East from Samarkand to Changan, the capital of ancient China from the Han, the Wei, the Sui and the Tang dynasty. The Sogdians traded not only in silk, but also in wood, woollen carpets, white cotton, glassware, Fergana and Kirgiz horses which the Chinese greatly desired, and fine armoured suits of iron made by their skilled iron-mongers. It is said that Tamerlane the Terrible insisted on wearing only Sogdiana armoured suits.

The Sogdians have largely disappeared or assimilated through wars and conquests and conversion to Islam. Only about three or four thousand Sogdians survive to this day in villages around Samarkand. They speak the Sogdian language but they cannot read their cursive, cuneiform-like writings.

Glossary

Amber Amber is not a rock mineral. It is of organic origin and is derived from the fossilized resin of pine trees. The best amber comes from the Baltic Region of what is now Soviet Russia. The colour of amber ranges from orange and yellow (beer-colour) to brown and even black. It is a very light substance and floats on saturated salt water. Imitation amber always sinks, and this is therefore a good test of real and imitation amber. Amber is soft, being rated at 2.5 on the Mohs scale of hardness. One can easily cut amber with a pocket knife. The various tribes in North Africa have always valued amber very highly.

Amethyst A variety of rock quartz, its colour ranges from lilac to rich royal purple, similar to the imperial purple on ancient Roman togas. Amethyst comes from various parts of the world, but the best is said to be of Siberian origin, while Brazil and Uruguay produce good quality amethyst. According to Dr Joel Arem, an authoritative mineralogist (see his *Gems and Jewellery*. New York: Ridge Press, 1975), amethyst was highly valued in ancient Israel, and it was used to decorate the breastplate of the High Priest. As a gem stone it wears well, being 7 on the Mohs scale of hardness. It turns red when reflected in artificial light.

Chalcedony A type of quartz mineral with tiny grains or fibrous and streaky crystals built into the matrix. It is also stained by natural pigmentation into colours of milky white, gray or shades of brown. It is a hard mineral whose fundamental matrix is quartz, or oxide of silicon. Quartz in its pure state is transparent and colourless, but when impurities get embedded into its matrix, it takes on a variety of colours and patterns. It is the most plentiful of mineral rocks on the surface of the earth, and in the form of chalcedony, it is the cheapest of gem materials.

Agate Another variety of quartz, characterized by fine grained patterns of colour banding and irregular cloudings. It is reddish brown and takes on a high polish. Sometimes the patterns on agate show fanciful shapes and images. The finest agates come from India, the U.S., Brazil and Mexico.

Jasper Yet another variety of quartz crystal. It is opaque and displays no regular patterns. It comes in shades of brown, red, green and yellow. Like other quartz compounds it is hard and dense and takes on a high, glossy polish.

Carnelian Carnelian (the old spelling was 'cornelian') is a chalcedony quartz whose colour ranges from brownish red to clear red. Traces of iron are responsible for the red line. It was one of the most popular of quartz mineral used in ancient times for making beads. But shaping beads out of carnelian pebbles was no easy matter because these quartz pebbles were 7 on the Mohs scale of hardness. Ancient bead-makers probably used corundum powder (emery abrasives) or quartz powder to rub these pebbles down to the required shapes and sizes.

Coral An organic marine product, coral is in fact the rock-hard skeletal structure of a variety of red corals (*corallium rubrum*) found in warm tropical seas. In its living state, coral grows into a small tree of irregular, red branches, the base of which is attached to some rock. The colour varies from light pink to blood red. Good quality coral is of uniform colour and it is dense enough to take on a high and gleaming polish. Oblate-shaped and tubular beads were the commonest forms of coral beads, and among the Tibetans and other Himalayan tribes coral was highly valued. The tribes of Benin in West Africa reserved the use of coral bead suits, head-dress and other insignias of authority to the 'Oba' or Chief. No other people were allowed the use of coral beads.

Jade Jade refers to two types of minerals, jadeite and nephrite. Jadeite is composed of sodium and aluminium silicate, while nephrite is made up of calcium and magnesium silicate. Jadeite is 7 on the Mohs scale of hardness while nephrite is slightly 'softer' at 6.5. Although jadeite is not as hard as corundum, it is very tough because its matrix is made up of interlocked crystals. Appearance-wise jadeite is crystalline and shiny, while nephrite has an oily look about it. Nephrite, especially the green variety, tends to be mottled with dark spots. White nephrite, known as 'mutton-fat' jade, has the texture of congealed fat.

While jade (both jadeite and nephrite varieties) has always been regarded as precious stones most highly valued by the Chinese, it was also used in ancient times in Central America by the Olmec, the Toltec, the Maya and Aztec tribes for their nobility and priestly classes. The Maoris of New Zealand also regarded jade as the most valuable of precious stones. Much of Chinese jade, however, came from countries outside of China, namely Turkestan, Burma and Siberia. In ancient China, most of the jades were nephrites and they came from Khotan. Mutton-fat white nephrite was mostly highly valued. Jadeite did not make its appearance in China until about the beginning of the eighteenth century. Emerald-green was the most highly valued colour. But lavender, red and brown jadeites were also imported – mainly from Burma.

The term 'carved jade' is actually a misnomer. Jade cannot be carved with the hardest steel chisels, saws, punches and drills. But jade can be polished, worn or rubbed down by using abrasives of fine quartz sand, crushed garnets (red sand) or black corundum (emery) powder. Hence, the 'carving' of a piece of jade boulder is a slow and tedious process requiring years of unremitting sanding and rubbing with abrasives.

Lapis-lazuli An opaque mineral rock made up of three different kinds of minerals, namely lazulite, pyrite and calcite, it is often speckled with golden flakes of iron pyrite. Fine lapis-lazuli has a deep violet-blue colour and traditionally the best of lapis came from Badakshan in Afghanistan. In fact the mines in Badakshan are said to have been mined continuously for over 6,000 years. The hardness of lapis-lazuli is 5.5–6 on the Mohs scale, so it is hard enough to take on a polished shine when processed into gems.

The Egyptians of Pharaonic times valued lapis-lazuli above gold, and only royalty and the priestly class could afford to wear jewellery studded with lapis-lazuli. Lapis was also used in all royal insignias, as the fabulous wealth of magnificent jewellery and royal emblems recovered from the tomb of Tut-ankh-amun showed. In fact, so great was the demand for lapis-lazuli, that Egyptian glass-workers devoted years of research to produce a type of blue faience beads which, to all intents and purposes, looked and felt like lapis-lazuli. Later the Phoenicians and Sumerians also learnt the secrets of making blue faience beads for export to Africa and Asia.

Ruby Ruby belongs to the variety of rock mineral called 'corundum', and all corundum crystals are composed of aluminium oxide. It is one of the hardest minerals, being rated at 9 on the Mohs scale of hardness. Pure corundum is a colourless and transparent-like rock crystal. But when traces of chromium are present in the corundum crystal, it takes on a brilliant red. Sapphire, blue sapphire that is, is corundum which has been adulterated with traces of iron and titanium. The finest rubies come from the Mogok area in Burma, and they are known as 'pigeon's blood rubies', because of their characteristic sparkling red. Modern gem rubies are faceted, but old rubies were rubbed into cabochon shapes, i.e. smooth, rounded and polished on top and unpolished on the underside.

Turquoise Next to lapis-lazuli, turquoise was a most highly valued gem in ancient times. It was treasured by people in the Middle East, Persia, Egypt and the Mediterranean countries. Turquoise is made up of copper aluminium phosphate and it belongs to the group of cryptocrystalline minerals which include jadeite, agate and nephrite. It is opaque and somewhat porous. But since it is about 6 on the Mohs scale, it can be polished to take a sheen. The best turquoise comes from north-eastern Iran and it is blue in colour (due largely to the presence of copper), but other varieties have a greenish cast. Turquoise has been made into beads from the earliest times.

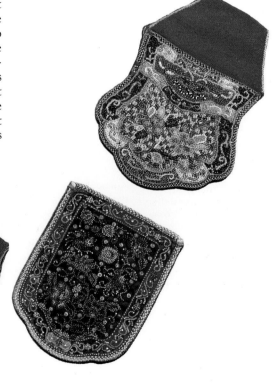

Bibliography

Aldred, Cyril. *Jewels of the Pharaohs*. New York: Ballantine Books, 1978.

Anderson, Frank J. *Riches of the Earth: Ornamental, Precious and Semi-precious stones*. New York: Windward, 1981.

Baker, A. C. 'An Historical Sketch of Malacca' in *Town and Port of Malacca*. Singapore: MPH, 1924.

Ball, J. Dyer. *Things Chinese*. Shanghai: Kelly and Walsh Ltd, 1925.

Bath, Virginia Churchill. *Needlework in America*. New York: Viking Press, 1979.

Boulnois, L. *The Silk Road*, transl. from the French by Dennis Chamberlain. George Allen & Unwin, 1966.

Breton, M. *China, Its Costumes, Arts, Manufactures*. Vol. IV. London: Stockdale, 1812. Transl. from French.

Bushell, S. W. *Chinese Art*, Vol. 2. London: His Majesty's Stationery Office, 1919.

Cable, Mildred, and Francesca French. *The Gobi Desert*. London: Hodder & Stoughton Ltd., 1942.

Cammann, Schulyer. 'Chinese Mandarin Squares'. *University of Pennsylvania Museum Bulletin*, Vol. 17, 1953.

Cammann, Schulyer. *China's Dragon Robes*. New York: Ronald Press, 1952.

Carter, Michael. *Crafts of China*. London: Aldus Books, 1977.

Chang, Queeny. *Memories of a Nonya*. Singapore: Eastern Universities Press, 1981.

Clark, Sir Kenneth. *Civilization*. London: B.B.C. and John Murray, 1969.

Coats, Peter. *Flowers in History*. Chapter on Peonies. London: Weidenfeld & Nicolson, 1970.

Confucius, *Analects*. D. C. Lau's translation. London: Penguin.

Cust, M. M., and Alford. *Needlework as Art*. New York & London: Garland Publishing Inc., 1978.

Desroaches-Noblecourt, Christiane. *Tutankhamen: The Life and Death of a Pharaoh*. London: Penguin, 1965.

Doolittle, Rev. Justus. *Vocabulary and Handbook of the Chinese Language*. 2 volumes. Foochow, China: Rozario Marcal & Co., 1872.

Erickson, Joan Mowat. *The Universal Bead*. New York: W. W. Norton & Co., 1969.

Feddersen, Martin. *Chinese Decorative Art: A Handbook for Collectors and Connoisseurs*. Transl. by Arthur Lane. London: Faber & Faber, 1961.

Ferguson, J. C. *Survey of Chinese Art*. Shanghai: The Commercial Press Ltd., 1939. Chapter 9, Textiles.

Fukai, Shinji. *Persian Glass*. Transl. by E. B. Crawford. New York and Tokyo: Weatherhill/Tankosha, 1977.

Gostelow, Mary. *Embroidery: Traditional Designs, Techniques and Patterns from all over the world*. London: Cavendish House, 1982.

Hedin, Sven. *History of the (Sino-British) Expedition in Asia*, 4 volumes. Stockholm, 1945. See Vol. 4.

Ho, Wing Meng. *Straits Chinese Porcelain*. Singapore: Times Books International, 1983.

Ho, Wing Meng. *Straits Chinese Silver*. Singapore: Times Books International, 1984.

Hudson, G. F. *Europe and China: A Survey of their Relations from the earliest times to 1800.* London: Edward Arnold, 1931.

Hughes, Graham. *Gems and Jewellery.* Oxford: Phaidon, 1978.

Jenyns, Soame. *Chinese Art (The Minor Arts)*, Vol. 4, Textiles. London: Oldbowrne Press, 1965.

Jones, Mary I. *A History of Western Embroidery.* London: Studio Vista.

Jourdain, M., and R. Soame Jenyns. *Chinese Export Art in Eighteenth Century.* London: Spring Book, 1967.

Kuntzsch, Ingrid. *A History of Jewels and Jewellery.* New York: St Martin's Press, 1981.

Life of the Emperors and Empresses in the Forbidden City. Beijing, China: China Travel and Tourism Press, 2nd edition, 1983.

Lockwood, M. S., and E. Glaister. *Art Embroidery: A Treatise on the Revived Practice of Decorative Needlework.* London: Marcus Ward & Co., 1878.

Mallakh, E., and C. Brackman. *The Gold of Tutankhamen.* New York: Newsweek Book, 1978.

New Archaelogical Finds in China, Vols. 1 and 2. Peking: Foreign Languages Press, 1973, 1978.

Piggott, Stuart. *Prehistoric India to 1000 B.C.* London: Penguin, 1950.

Priest, Alan, and Pauline Simon. *Chinese Textiles.* New York Metropolitan Museum Exhibition – 1931–32.

Selections of Masterworks in the Collection of the National Palace Museum. Taiwan: 1974.

Seyd, Mary. *Introducing Beads.* London: B. T. Batsford Ltd., 1973.

Shellabear, W. G. *An English–Malay Dictionary.* Singapore: Malayan Publishing House, 1916.

Sleen, Van der, W. G. N. *A Handbook of Beads.* Liege: Musée du Verre, 1967.

Snook, Barbara. *Embroidery Stitches.* London: B. T. Batsford Ltd., 1972.

Stein, Sir Marc Auriel. *Ancient Khotan: Detailed Report of Archaelogical Exploration in Chinese Turkestan.* 2 vols. Oxford: Clarendon, 1907.

Stein, Sir Marc Auriel. *Serinda: Detailed Report of the Explorations in Central Asia and Westernmost China.* 4 vols. Oxford, Clarendon.

Straits Chinese Monthly. Singapore, 1931 and 1933 issues.

Traditional Chinese Textile Designs. New York: Dover Publications, 1980.

Tsien, Tsuen-hsiun. *Written on Bamboo and Silk: The Beginnings of Chinese Books and Inscriptions.* Chicago: The University of Chicago Press, 1962.

Vlekke, B. H. M. *Nusantara.* Cambridge: Cambridge University Press, 1944.

Volbach, W. Fritz. *Early Decorative Textiles.* Paul Hamlyn, 1969.

Vollmer, John E. *In the Presence of the Dragon Throne.* Toronto: Royal Ontario Museum, 1977.

Wray, L. 'Native Arts and Handicrafts' in *Twentieth Century Impressions of British Malaya*, 1908.

Wright, Arnold. *Twentieth Century Impressions of British Malaya.* London: Lloyd's Greater Britain Publishing Co., 1908.

Index